WHAT THEY SAY ABO

Over the last three decades, Dean Fraser has become one of the world's leading advocates of dowsing as a means of connecting to our own intuition and is also a passionate teacher of meditation and holistic lifestyles – PSYCHIC NEWS

The author's quest for metaphysical growth has seen him travel across two continents in search of truth, network with fellow seekers of enlightenment and visit sacred sites to attune with their energies – BODYMINDSOUL.COM

Dean was very interactive with the audience afterwards and from that, he has offered to come back to do a session on how to meditate. A direct request from the audience – EVENT HOST

Dean sees his mission in life to spread some much-needed laughter and love in this world - INDIE SHAMAN MAGAZINE

Although the author and publisher have made every effort to ensure that the information in this book was correct at press time, the author and publisher do not assume and hereby disclaim any liability to any party for any loss, damage, or disruption caused by errors or omissions, whether such errors or omissions result from negligence, accident, or any other cause. This book is not intended as a substitute for the medical advice of healthcare professionals. The reader should regularly consult their chosen medical professional in matters relating to his/her health and particularly with respect to any symptoms that may require diagnosis or medical attention.

> Love is quite simply the most powerful creative force, self-healing energy and gift to wellbeing that exists...
>
> Dean Fraser

The Magic Of Holistic Living

A Guide To Happiness & Wellbeing

Dean Fraser

In this life we live by our free will choice
Be quiet to listen to our own inner voice

CONTENTS

Introduction

I often have interviewers ask me how much of these modalities on holistic living teach do I personally use? Where am I in my own life and is every day perfect?

I am on the same journey as you and can only endeavour to be the best version of myself. I fully appreciate some of these things are far easier to talk about than practically realise. I also understand how some of my wisdoms will speak to you more than others.

I have been on an intentional path of self-growth since the late 1980's, like all of us I have life's challenges to deal with, the crucial difference is in perspective. Whereas once up a time I would have see-sawed from one emotional extreme to another, now my approach is more centred and balanced. I attribute this directly to using the methods you will be reading about throughout our personal journey together in this book.

Dean Fraser

The Healing Journey To Self-Love

Lack of self-love remains the source of enumerable psychological issues and when left unchecked goes on to create all too real cardiac related physical challenges to deal with. Self-love is essential if we hope to gain mastery of the game of life.

Whatever achievements we wish to accomplish, if they are worthy of our precious time and energy, deserve to be invested with a large healthy dose of love; and self-love is essential to achieve any kind of lasting peace of mind. Love for ourselves turbo-charges life with transformational energy permeating through our entire reality.

I acted as my own guinea pig to discover the road to self-love! Initially by following my intuition; one step at a time I developed a new paradigm based around discovering my Happy Point.

Happy Point modality is a path to self-love I teach today in my seminars. I developed this directly from out of my own experiences.

THE HAPPY POINT MODALITY

Planting the smallest acorn of self-love can grow into your inner oak tree of certainty. The following exercise can trigger the flowering of self-love within our hearts: -

1. Find somewhere you will be undisturbed for the next twenty minutes. Sit in a relaxing chair or lay down if that feels more comfortable. In a relaxed way begin to concentrate all your attention solely upon your breathing. Observe how your body feels. Is there tension anywhere? Gently move your shoulders or any other tense area of your body to release that tightness, as you continue to centre all your attention completely on your breathing.

2. You are embarking on an inner journey deep into your inner essence to discover your Happy Point.

3. Gently ponder all the many facets making up your uniqueness of the person you are. As you are relaxing into the sensation, choose to focus your attention on one part of who you are which you feel happy with. And it doesn't matter how small or seemingly unimportant this single facet may appear to be. One brilliant fraction of all that makes up the whole of you, which works so well for you and always makes you feel at ease and happy. One selected piece of the myriad of the you of you, which sits so comfortably within you.

4. Enjoy the warmth of the feeling as you concentrate and focus all of your attention entirely on how this wonderful part of

you makes you feel when you ponder deeply upon it. Spend at least five minutes keeping this feel-good factor central to your emotions.

5. Next pick a colour to represent this feel-good sensation. Apply a colour to that feeling! And it does not matter what colour that might be. One which just seems right to your intuition is the perfect choice. This wonderful feel-good sensation is forever now inexorably linked together with what will be your Happy Point Colour! Spend some moments strongly visioning this colour as you bask in the warmth of the feeling.

6. So is it possible bring that warm feeling into other parts of your life? Wouldn't it be amazing to feel this fabulous across the entire spectrum of you? You can make this happen...

7. Still focussing all of your attention on those amazing feel-good sensations together with the colour this emotional high is associated with...gently and naturally begin to re-align your attention to now think about some other aspect of yourself which you sense needs some definite work. Maybe this is something you dislike in your own reactions to situations that has become too engrained within you or a habitual pattern of thinking you empathically know has outlived its time through feeling like emotional baggage you have carried around with you for far too long.

8. It is important here to concentrate solely upon only one area of your life for this session; one area you sense needs work.

9. As you ponder all the emotions associated with this more challenging aspect of you, gradually and naturally start to overlay this feeling with the colour you associated with those beautiful, feel-good sensations you experienced only a few moments ago. All you see in your mind is your Happy Point colour completely overlaying the challenging issue. Feel this! You deserve to really feel this!!!

10. Return to your normal waking state once you sense you have done enough for this session.

What is happening here is the start of an inner transformational process. You are self-healing to welcome self-love into your life. Re-programming old paradigms; healing them one by one using your Happy Point Colour.

We all have choices on which paths we take in life, we are constantly presented with potential directions. And you possess your own personal map to self-love. Please take the time to use it.

We are all perfect at being ourselves, we just need reminding how. Then our higher-love, our connection to source grows stronger throughout every day of our life.

Any time we find ourselves facing a challenging situation or tackling a potentially toxic person, if we stay focussed on the colour associated with our Happy Point, we bring self-love into the situation. And nothing is more empowering than love!

You might even like to reinforce this process further by wearing or keeping the colour you associate with your Happy Point around your immediate environment.

The more you practice this the easier it gets, and a natural part of the process is you experience the beginning of a transformed approach and positive new outlook to life unfolding for you.

Pendulum Dowsing & Spiritual Healing

Pendulums work in situations where rods or twig would be difficult or impossible to apply. They are especially useful within the fields of dowsing lists, psychic development, map dowsing, spiritual healing and testing food. Most of these applications would become unnecessarily complicated with applying rods or twigs; a pendulum however is ideal.

Pendulums are also usefully portable; they easily fit into a pocket or small bag. Taken out to use as required and then easily stowed away again until next time. They are also discreet, avoiding the interested attention the rod or twig dowser usually attracts.

When landscape dowsing, if the weather is inclement, we can use our pendulum to dowse maps from the comfort of our car or indeed even our favourite armchair.

Another advantage of opting for a pendulum becomes clear when asking questions from dowsing. We get an extremely specific and consistent response from a dowsing pendulum. The skill can sometimes be in later interpreting these results within the context of our lives.

Which style of pendulum to go for is down to personal choice. There are myriads of options available; from pendulums made from metals such as brass or copper, crystal or semi-precious gemstones, and through to a variety different natural wood options. We can even craft a pendulum for ourselves using a plumb bob on a piece of cord or choose a heavy old-style door key, again suspended on a cord. As long as the weight hangs straight and true, we have a practical pendulum.

PURE DOWSING

You want to ensure your dowsing will be pure and real from day one. This exercise will guarantee this is the case.

A pendulum works by responding in movements to specific questions asked of it. These movements will be in one of three different ways. The given answer will always be YES, NO or MAYBE.

So every time we ask any kind of question our pendulum will move in one of these three ways and we arrive at our answer. The specific direction a pendulum moves in answer to a question varies from person to person. There is no right or wrong here. Movements can include clockwise or counter-clockwise rotation, forward and backward swinging, side to side swinging, diagonal swinging or even ovoid rotation.

You can establish your own dowsing pendulum responses through this exercise.

Take a piece of card and evenly spaced write YES, NO and MAYBE on it, and cut them out to make three identical sized squares of card.

Find somewhere quiet to sit where there is no chance of being disturbed. A place far away from everyday distractions such as children, partners, televisions, radios, computers, phones or any of the other thousand and one things that could spoil your concentration.

Take the pendulum in your projective hand, which is the one you usually write with. Hold it by pinching the chain or cord between your thumb and forefinger, allowing about 15cm (6 inches) to hang freely before reaching the pendulum (No need to measure this, just approximately is fine!), wrap any remaining length of cord inside your hand.

Hold your pendulum over the piece of card with YES written on it. While focusing on the writing say out loud or in your head "What is my YES response?"

Be patient as this might take a few seconds to get a response to start off with. Your pendulum will start to slowly vibrate and then gently at first move in a specific direction.

Let it move in this direction for at least a minute once it is freely swinging. This can seem a little eerie at first, watching the pendulum swinging of its own accord. From this moment on this direction will now always be your YES answer to any question you may ask of your pendulum.

Having firmly established your YES response, logically we move on to NO next. Hold your pendulum over the piece of card with NO written on it. Ask the question out loud or in your head "What is my NO response?" and slowly the pendulum will take on a movement in a definite direction, but different from your YES direction.

Once again let it swing freely for at least a minute. We have now also your established NO response to any question you may ask of your pendulum.

At this point, by using your pendulum to ask questions you will be able to establish a definite YES or NO response.

MAYBE comes into play if a question you ask does not have a readily available or obvious YES or NO response answer.

A MAYBE response enables us to ask the question again in another way for a definite YES or NO response. Or wait until some later date or time to have another go. Then again we sometimes have to accept that there are simply some things we are not yet meant to know. This can often happen when using a pendulum for attempting the prediction of future outcomes of events in life - as there are often so many unforeseen variables which can come into play, a specific YES or NO is impossible.

Take the card with MAYBE written on it. Naturally, this works exactly the same as when you established your YES and NO responses. Holding your pendulum over the MAYBE card and ask out loud or to yourself "What is my MAYBE response?" Once again your pendulum will take on a new movement, different from your YES and NO.

Let it carry on swinging for at least a minute to be sure of your directional movement and from this moment this will then always be your MAYBE response.

Once you have completed these exercises you will have all you need to get started with dowsing. You have your YES, NO or MAYBE response to any question you care to ask and your pendulum will always give you one of those three answers.

SPIRITUAL HEALING

Although dowsing with a pendulum can be used in myriads of applications to provide quick responses to more or less any question, it lends itself particularly well to spiritual healing.

The art, as always, is knowing the right questions to ask. This book aims to help you to help yourself and others, through instilling the confidence to expand into your own dowsing capabilities.

Okay, I guess before we go any further it would be useful for me to talk about dowsing in a more general sense, to set the scene for our journey together through this book.

Let's start with what dowsing isn't:

- Dowsing isn't a parlour game or trick for our own or other's amusement.
- Dowsing isn't infallible, especially when dealing with matters impacting upon health do be sure to validate any findings with your chosen healthcare provider.
- Dowsing isn't the answer to everything. My whole philosophy is to help my readers develop their own intuition to trust what is often referred to as our gut instinct. Our pendulum is the perfect tool to help us achieve this.

Dowsing is:

- A method of bypassing our conscious minds to get straight to the heart of a matter.
- Insightful and often surprising in the answers we receive.
- Invaluable in helping ourselves and others.
- Gives us an answer to question we ask of our pendulum.

I am an intuitive healer. Having first discovered my ability when quite small, assuming everyone did this I became confused when dawning realisation hit me this is far from the case. What might have been a little isolating from others in fact turned out differently as I gradually learned to tune-out from the constant stream of energy I picked-up from those around me, sensing any maladies they may be afflicted with.

My first healing for another person didn't involve dowsing. We visited my mother's parents regularly. On one such occasion my mum's mum, we called her Nana, had a debilitating headache. The kind which would have required strong painkillers to deal with if she actually had any in the house, unfortunately she didn't (or perhaps fortunately, depending on how we view these things). Nana sat there in her usual armchair, with the blinds drawn tight shut, reducing the glare from the painful daylight. Instinctively I placed a small hand on her forehead; she winced as even my child's gentle touch must have seemed to her like a heavy weight. I quietly asked her to sit still and wait. Family watched on, as over the course of around fifteen minutes Nana's headache entirely disappeared. And presently, with the blinds now open, she became well enough to pick up her discarded newspaper to begin the crossword (her favourite pastime). My parents thankfully were open-minded enough not to make too big a deal or fuss about their toddler spontaneously healing his grandparent's migraine. My services though were thereafter called-upon if any member of my immediate family might find themselves challenged with pain or fever; and invariably my intuitive intervention did help.

Over the years I also developed an equally intuitive code of ethics relating to healing for others, meaning under no circumstances would I ever offer any kind of healing unless directly asked for. I feel I have no right to directly interfere in the lives of others if they don't wish me to, and if their path means they need to go through certain learning experiences along the way, it is equally their right to do so. I still live by this same code quite a few decades on...I feel it is a good code to live by generally. By all means offering help if asked for, yet otherwise respecting the right of everyone to go through their own experience on this journey called life, the same as we would wish.

As I say in all my dowsing workshops, in teaching people to dowse I always feel I am giving them the keys to a better understanding of themselves and the World around them. I still get excited with them the first time it works and share a renewed awe for this unexplainable phenomenon.

DOWSING & HEALING

There is a school of thought suggesting anything at all we are experiencing in terms of illness or dis-ease, will have its root origins in the emotions we have been habitually feeling.

Spiritual healing is a non-intrusive way of releasing emotional blockages and getting us out of the comfort zone of self-defeating mindsets. We can use dowsing to confirm what intuition suspects and then offer a healing, later to re-dowse and see if further healing will be necessary.

Emotional blockages can form in many ways, often through a consistent suppression of unexpressed emotions about a situation or due to poor self-created energy as a result of stress and feelings of helplessness.

Healings can be practised with the client present or as a distant healing.

WHAT IS SPIRITUAL HEALING?

Spiritual healing is helping our minds or bodies to heal themselves. After al,I isn't that essentially what any healing is? For sure if we go along the conventional route to health, taking ourselves off to a GP and embracing orthodox medicine, it is still our own body which is healing for itself. Prescribed drugs or medication simply won't work if you or I believe they will be effective. Conversely there have been well documented cases of individuals making full recoveries from serious illnesses, while in reality having been taking nothing more than a placebo pill, their trust in its effectiveness being enough to bring about healing.

I believe in the power of dowsing; however a little common sense is prudent here. If you and I have no formal medical training we won't understand the complexities of how the human body works in the same way that a doctor would. Therefore, the dowser who is attempting to diagnose a serious medical condition in someone, without the benefit of those years of vocational training, cannot know what is really going on with their illness and where their symptoms are originating from. The art, as always, is in knowing the correct questions to ask; in this case without that medical training this is impossible. A doctor clearly does know the right questions and makes their diagnosis based on complete knowledge of sympathetic symptoms, using their learned expertise in interpreting them.

Spiritual healing most often deals with emotional blockages, those which if left undealt with can cause all too real psychological and physical symptoms to manifest. When I practise a direct healing, I can feel these blockages, and precisely in which part of the body they are located. After dowsing to confirm my finding, I apply extra energy of my own, with the intention to release the person's blockage of energy to flow freely once again through the meridians of their body.

This is rarely hands-on these days. When it is, I will hold my hand approximately 20cm over the affected area. I dowse the area beforehand, to confirm my intuitive feelings by asking of my pendulum *"is this where the energy blockage is located?"* until I can narrow my answers down to a specific location in their body. After the healing I re-dowse to further ask *"is the blockage now clear?"* A session lasts about fifteen minutes. I have been told what we healers do is akin to acupuncture or acupressure, but without any physical contact.

If we are healing for another we can use either the hand we usually write with (our projective hand) or a combination of both hands, depending upon what feels right to us. Personally, I generally use my right hand, but there are no right or wrongs here, you need to do this whatever way your intuition guides you.

We visualize white light passing down our own arm and out of our palm directly into the area where our client is experiencing the emotional blockage. This needs to feel relaxed, never forced, to continue for up to fifteen minutes (any longer would be offering too much energy) and only once a day for the individual client.

Some have asked if these sessions make me feel tired afterwards. Not these days really too much at all, in the earlier part of my development for sure though as I tended more to absorb maladies rather than clearing them. Back in those earlier days I was usually using my left hand (my receptive hand) for healing sessions, absorbing the malady to help heal. This is not recommended, by the way, far better to clear the blockage for a client so they heal for themselves, rather than personally empathically taking on their pain, even if it is usually quickly dissipated from our own bodies.

Using one's own energy to help another does require a few ground rules from those such as you or I, who are the healer

- We must be free from stress and anger.

- We need to remain balanced and centred throughout the healing session.

- We cannot allow ourselves to become too empathic to the client; otherwise taking on their emotional state for ourselves is all too real a possibility. We need to remain slightly detached to reduce the chances of this happening.

- All kinds of deep-seated emotions can be brought bubbling to the surface during a healing and we definitely need to be prepared for this trauma being allowed the freedom to be released at long last and it can seem shocking to witness. It is not uncommon to see clients crying uncontrollably or looking utterly shocked – this is quite normal and an essential part of their healing process. You might like to practise a further healing for them the next day, helping them in reaching some internal balance to process the new experiences they are passing through. Things do thankfully usually settle down again quickly, after all the trauma causing the emotional blockage might well have been ignored for years or even decades! That the client has sought help, as their body is telling them in no uncertain terms it is unhappy; suggest it is now time to lay the issue afflicting them to rest...

Angus I had known for many years and he is an extremely private person. Sharing with others anything he might personally feel afflicted with is never easy for Angus...his priority is helping others, placing his own needs last.

For two months he had been experiencing what felt like a constriction in his throat, he said to him it was like some unseen entity might be gently attempting to throttle him! He did his best to ignore what he tried to persuade himself to be only a slight inconvenience, doing his level best to continue with life as usual. I knew I might complete a healing for Angus, if given the opportunity; he simply needed to request my help, otherwise I could do nothing. After personally witnessing one of these episodes and being quite obviously not in the slightest bit phased by what I saw before me, led Angus to finally ask what I thought might be happening to him and further rather reluctantly request if I might be able to help him.

I had a pretty good idea what the issue might be, as usual when offering a healing I told him I offer no guarantees regarding results, nevertheless promised some healing on his behalf. I immediately used my pendulum to establish beyond doubt the exact location of his emotional blockage, and further asked out loud the question *"can I help Angus?"* to happily get my Yes response. To be honest this question was more for the benefit of Angus, as I already knew that I could help!

Dowsing in private later confirmed my suspicions as to what Angus found himself having to contend with. His case wasn't that unusual in my experience, I instinctively sensed why he had an emotional blockage, using my pendulum validated my initial intuitive feeling. This blockage affected him physically and would only intensify if left unchecked. Quite commonplace in those who seek me out, I can deal with them generally comparatively easily.

Angus possessed a particularly strong emotional blockage in his throat chakra and ultimately it took an unprecedented three healing sessions to totally eradicate it. In his case this blockage had gradually built up over a period of over a year because of unexpressed feelings of frustration, buried deep inside of him and never allowed the opportunity to be verbally expressed. This physically manifested as his throat issues and the all too real feeling of choking, a throat chakra blockage having developed due to him feeling unable to communicate his inner feelings to anyone.

Having once worked in senior management within local government, due to downsizing his department, Angus had found himself unexpectedly made redundant one year before. I suggested his need to heal himself through finally confronting this traumatic situation from a year ago he had never dealt with or talked about to anyone. I told him that in order to be practically able continue in his self-confessed quest to assist others, he needed to firstly help himself by letting go of his past career and his own self-image which went with it. This had become practically essential in order to move on with his life...he talked for several hours to me about all his deeply buried sense of loss as his much loved career ended, and his utter lacking in motivation to start all over again.

Finally cleared of the emotional blockage, Angus wanted purpose to his life once more and live taking due care of his own interests. If he existed in a happy, fit and healthy state, he would find it far easier to help others. He commenced sincerely seeking a new direction from life and in due course opportunity came along for him to work within a career close not only his own front door, but definitely even more close to his heart.

Angus found the ideal employment managing the drop-in centre for the homeless he had previously been volunteering at for the last year.

DISTANT HEALING

Most of my own healing for others these days is done over a distance, this way I get to help many more people, the majority of who I usually never physically meet.

When I practise an absent spiritual my actual method is often identical, it usually differs only really in the sense of what I am treating.

The email which arrived one particular day once again confirmed what I firmly believe, that there are some people who remain destined to cross our paths for a pre-determined reason. Even if to begin with we have no idea what this reason might be!

The woman in question getting in touch was definitely a serendipitous happening. In my positive reply to her questioning email, I asked how I might help. Lucy took the opportunity to tell me her story, to share things for the first time which she felt most others around her would likely find a little too weird.

Lucy wasn't just in another country from where I am based; she was on a different continent and indeed, located on more or less the other side of the world. She was deeply unhappy, lacking energy and motivation to change anything in her life – whilst paradoxically knowing on one level she definitely needed to do precisely that. She felt lethargic, and her underlying worry was that she could have some serious illness all the health professionals had missed during her frequent visits to them for consultation.

Promising I would do several distant healings for her, here I possessed an opportunity to in fact stretch my own ability to the outer limits. To afford a healing session for someone who not only lived on the opposite side of the globe, but also in a completely different time-zone; I found myself fascinated to see how it might all work out for both of us!

My pendulum as usual allowed me to get to the heart of the matter for Lucy. When we don't actually have our client right there in front of us to ask them questions or watch their body language as they respond, our pendulum proves invaluable. Here are some of the questions I asked relating to this case:

- Has Lucy got some as yet undiagnosed illness? (answer Maybe)
- Does Lucy have emotional blockages? (No)
- One emotional blockage? (No)
- Multi-layered emotional blockages? (No)
- Are my intuitive senses of what is causing Lucy these issues for correct? (Yes)
- Will a healing session from here be able to help Lucy? (Yes)

I commenced my distant healing session, more to get a sense of exactly how I might help Lucy and what was literally her issue. Please understand when one does a healing we cannot read the client's mind, all their personal and private thoughts remain just that, private. What I did feel strongly coming back from Lucy was her physical body crying-out in distress. The strongest sense she needed to change her eating habits and like now!

I am not a qualified nutritionist, what I have though is three decades of experience in being vigilant in what I choose to take into my body by way of food and drink; plus, much networking with those more qualified than myself in matters of nutrition. Lucy confirmed by email, although she was vegetarian, her diet consisted mainly of convenience fast-food and the only liquid she took all day were soda drinks. No wonder she experienced mood swings and energy issues!

My suggestion was firstly to reduce her sugar intake as much as she felt comfortable with for the moment; then secondly, start eating more pure grains such as oats, brown rice, rye, etc; and fresh organic vegetables. Finally, ditch the soda and replace it with primarily water and bancha tea if she fancied something else.

My advice is always intuitive; to be confirmed by my dowsing and often I offer a cleansing of emotional blockages in a healing session. With Lucy this became a more urgent requirement for her to change her lifestyle as quickly as she could, I did sense if she continued along the same life path, she would get quite sick, quite soon.

Long story short – Lucy gradually took my suggestions on board and slowly started to get her life back. Over the course of six months she weened herself off all the sugary food and drinks completely. Happily, she also feels far more in-balance within her moods, and generally now possesses more energy and enthusiasm for life.

HOW IS IT DONE THEN?

For the first time I now share the inner workings of how I undertake a distant healing session.

Initially I concentrate all of my attention on the potential client, usually this is done while looking at the email they have sent me, giving myself a sense of exactly what I might be dealing with during a possible healing. I don't automatically offer my services when I get contacted, I get many requests each year for help and to get involved in every single case would leave me no time to live my own life. If this initial sense of the potential client offers up something really obvious which doesn't require a healing session, I immediately email them back with relevant suggestions and leave it at that. If I believe I can help in a more direct sense, based on my intuition I ask for more information.

Then comes pendulum dowsing! Asking pertinent questions allows me to get Yes, No or Maybe responses. Affording me a greater understanding of how the healing needs to proceed.

I lay horizontal, allowing my body to completely relax. This is a form of meditation. Following my earlier tuning-into the client when having their email in front of me, I now use the same path to connect to their spiritual essence. Instantly I can sense if I either need to directly help them with a healing to release emotional blocks or, as in the case with Lucy, get back to them with suggestions on how they might help themselves.

There are as many varied methods of spiritual healing as there are healers out there. You don't have to follow mine, yet why not give it a go; you might find it works for you just fine!

Start with someone you know, tell them you are wishing to develop the ability to distant heal; ask their permission to allow themselves to be your first experiment in healing. If they are open minded enough (and why would you even ask anyone who isn't?!) they will usually say Yes.

Follow the procedure I already outlined; you crucially need to remain relaxed during the process. And please bear in mind, even with the best intentions in the world, sometimes we simply cannot do a healing for another. It has happened with me a few times and I am sure it will again in the future. If it doesn't seem to be working first time out, don't stress it...we are none of us born experts, we become this with practise. So, have another go on another day, see if it works better then. Sooner or later it will happen. I believe we are all born with an innate ability to heal ourselves; and because we are all composed of energy, we can use our self-healing ability to help others.

My advice is not to gamble with your or anyone else's health, if feeling consistently unwell, please go seek professional medical attention. Dowsing should <u>never</u> be used to self-diagnose or diagnose illness in anyone else (unless you are actually a qualified doctor and even then, check your results conventionally please before treating your patient!).

Dowsing will also not cure your broken leg by itself, although having said that it will confirm your leg is broken ,if there was ever any doubt in the matter, then go get it professionally set!

AFTERWORD

In healing for others, my belief is that the forces that govern our Universe and in fact our own higher selves, only allows knowledge we are currently evolved enough to comprehend to come into our sphere of activity. If our consciousness is not ready to take on certain wisdoms we will not be able to obtain them.

Evolvement comes from our living, making mistakes which are not really mistakes but learning, walking our talk and sometimes tripping up along the way a few times before we finally get the message about what we need in order to grow. Shedding our ingrained patterns of behaviour as we progress through life; rather like a snake sheds its own skin to renew itself.

Knowing more about ourselves and our interconnectedness with all things is the start of true wisdom. If we choose to attempt to grow as people, we have a great tool to help us, our dowsing pendulum.

Crystals And You

I first became aware of the inherent power of crystals in the early 1990's. Until this moment I confess, although already a student of what I would come to think of as metaphysics, crystals were not something I had really given much thought to. Up until that point I never felt inclined to explore for myself crystal energy. A paradigm shift awaited me...

My introduction to crystals effectively came as a result of my dowsing. I read books. And I mean a lot of books! I still read, but nothing like at the level of intensity I did back then. I absorbed all of this knowledge like a sponge.

By and by I commenced reading the extensive series of books based around the readings of somnambulist mystic Edgar Cayce. Working my way through these writings I found myself intrigued by his frequent mentions of the healing power of gems and crystals. Particularly Cayce's references to crystals and the lost lands of Atlantis and Lemuria caught my attention. My interest suitably piqued, my next project was to learn more of these crystals and what bringing them into my own life might do for me.

In those days before the internet, finding metaphysical suppliers meant buying the kinds of magazines they might be found to advertise in. Such a magazine showed there to be a crystal shop located one hour's drive from me. Off I went to see what I would see.

I recognised some of the crystals from all the books I had been reading. I bought an amethyst cluster, a rose quartz tumble stone and quartz point. Little did I know what awaited me!

Within a year I had set up a wholesale business, The Strawberry Crystal, supplying shops, healing centres and educational centres in my native UK, also Sweden, Spain and Canada.

During the course of two decades my knowledge of crystals organically expanded and grew. I got asked to give talks at spiritual centres on the healing potential of crystals and this practically sealed the fate of The Strawberry Crystal. I found myself enjoying sharing my enthusiasm for crystals with an interested audience far more personally rewarding than running a wholesale business. I made what turned out to the easy choice, closing my business to focus my energy on delivering talks as my future career.

Whilst there are so many books dealing with which crystals to wear for optimum health, I felt you would appreciate what energetic changes we bring to homes or work space by placing them within our environment.

CRYSTALS IN THE HOME AND AT WORK

There are numerous ways that crystals can be utilized to benefit our environment. They can be used to help clear negativity, create a relaxing room or energise the atmosphere. Protection is another way. We will deal with each of these uses in turn.

CLEANSING NEGATIVITY

The best crystal for maintaining a positive environment is a nice large Amethyst Cluster. Simply place it in the room you wish to treat and leave it do its stuff. Can be used for protecting against the Electro-Magnetic Energy that is emitted by computers and televisions by placing a small Amethyst Cluster adjacent to them or alternatively adopt a Spider Plant (Chlorophytum comosum) as this is believed to happily absorb potentially harmful EMF radiations and still thrive.

RELAXATION

Rose Quartz is used to create a relaxing room. Usually sold as solid pieces of rock, this beautiful pink stone is also known as the Love Stone. Use a piece at least one kilo in size to treat a normal room. This is a gorgeous stone to have around the home. Place tumble-polished pieces of Rose Quartz in a crystal bowl to spread the feeling of love in a personal space.

ENERGIZING

You might wish to create an environment full of energized vibrations; for this a Quartz Crystal Cluster or Large Quartz Point is ideal. Perfect for use in an office as well; reputed to inspire brilliant ideas and allow people to function to the best of their ability. Quartz is used for developing latent psychic ability, so perfect for inspiring intuition and creative thought.

PROTECTION

We all wish our homes to feel safe and relaxing places to be. For a little extra help in creating your perfect retreat from the World, a large piece of marble is the crystal of choice, get larger decorative marble items or beautiful tumble-polished pieces and place them in a crystal bowl.

PRECIOUS CRYSTALS AND STONES

The way the majority of us wear crystals is as jewellery; engagement or wedding rings, beads and earrings, amongst obviously many other forms of jewellery. As they are often worn continuously it is clearly vitally important these harmonize with us. A little research in choosing the right gemstone to wear every day upon your person must be worth the effort...

The following list offers the widely held beliefs regarding the healing energy attached to most popular gems.

AMBER

Highly valued for its legendary magical properties, Amber has powerful warm energy. As this gem is millions of year's old fossilized tree resin, it is thought to allow a connection to our past lives and the wisdom of our ancestors. Also, said to enhance beauty when worn as jewellery. Wearing Amber is believed to be magically protective, especially in combination with Jet.

AMETHYST

Regarded as one of the great healing stones and is also used for opening up psychic abilities. Amethyst is believed to be protective against viruses and act as a general health promoting gemstone. Amethyst connects to the third eye and is used in meditation to gain insight and access higher wisdoms.

AQUAMARINE

Traditionally used to offer protection when travelling over water, to offer a connection to ancient sea deities and therefore reduce the symptoms of seas sickness. Aquamarine is one of the Goddess Stones to engender soul harmony within the feminine aspect of creation, regardless of gender. A beautiful gemstone to wear for soothing, gentle energy.

DIAMOND

No self-respecting section on crystals could overlook this quintessential gemstone. Has a reputation as a powerful money attracting gem. Knights of old wore Diamonds, as thought to render the wearer invincible. The facets of the cut gemstone reflect light, and this is symbolic of the way Diamonds reflect back the negative thoughts or actions of others.

JET

Often worn in conjunction with Amber by those taking part in shamanic magical rituals. Jet is thought to offer a way of achieving alternate levels of consciousness and protection against psychic attack. Is a warming stone, used by healers to treat pain associated with coldness.

KUNZITE

Thought to help with treatment of PMT, believed to help balance hormone production. This pink stone is said to open the mind to higher love and enable full physical expression without inhibitions or anxiety.

MALACHITE

Said to be a greatly powerful healing stone; one that should be treated with respect. When worn or carried it will draw love towards it. Malachite is believed to ensure t we remain in perfect health always. This is another stone of the Goddess, which can benefit any gender.

MOLDAVITE

Has been called the extra-terrestrial stone of transformation. Moldavite is translucent green coloured glassy meteor deposits found in only one area on the planet, in the Czech Republic. Prior to this millennium, Moldavite was used in meditation for transcendentally otherworldly experiences.

After the millennium its energy changed forever. Now, Moldavite is a fiercely protective stone – ensuring the wearer or carrier immunity to the challenging behaviour of others. In fact, has a reputation for removing anyone toxic from our lives.

OPAL

Used as a stone of confidence. Favoured by those who need to speak in public and are involved in the performing arts, said to reduce stage fright. Has a reputation for being unlucky, although there is no real evidence to support this theory, perhaps it originates from the fact Opals, if unworn, can dry out and become ruined, although it does take an exceedingly long time for this to occur. Opal is a beautiful stone that deserves to be worn and treasured. Caution is advised purchasing Opal jewellery as much of the stones actually only a slim slice of Opal, with a clear Quartz cabochon placed over. Pure Opal costs a lot of any currency we could mention, so if your potential purchase is surprisingly well priced, chances are it will be covered with a Quartz cabochon.

SUNSTONE

This quite rare gemstone is said to be a happy stone, inducing feelings of well-being. In healing is used to warm up cold or unfeeling personalities and enable them to enjoy life and being alive. Unsurprisingly Sunstone connects to the life-giving energy of the Sun.

TOPAZ BLUE

Traditionally set into silver and worn as a protective amulet. For boosting confidence and allowing us to realise our full potential. Trust your own judgement rather than being influenced by the deeds or actions of others. Topaz Blue is thought to keep the skin looking youthful.

TOURMALINE BLACK

Thought to be excellent for purifying our physical system. Is believed to encourage a positive outlook on life and an optimistic view, rather than fault finding. Encourages one to personally do something to improve a situation or help the attitude of any person, rather than feeling sorry for oneself. Said to be helpful to those with a tendency towards depression, lifting the mood.

TURQUOISE

Held sacred in many cultures and has a long history of mystical use that goes back into the mists of time. Pure wisdom which can be tuned into through meditation. The life force energy. Wear Turquoise to generate feelings of well-being and open the mind to the wisdom of the ages.

Happiness Empowerment

The advice I offer in my books and those I share in my talks represent my own truths as they evolved during my several decades of experience. I would certainly never profess to possess exclusive rights to the truth. For me to expect every single word I say or write to apply to everyone I meet or who reads my books, regardless of their own personal story, would be overbearingly arrogant on my part.

Use those of my truths for yourself which resonate enough to feel like sound concepts to you; then see where working them takes you.

WHAT DO YOU THINK?

We all listen to this constant stream of thoughts going on in our heads. We identify with this voice in our head as being the 'true us' and naturally automatically tend to believe everything we tell ourselves through this constant inner chatter of ours.

Yet how can we be sure though that every single one of these thoughts or inner conversations of is genuinely true? Most of us believe everything we think all the time. Accepting all these thoughts are concrete facts.

How about this one though?

When you were sixteen years old, assuming you are not sixteen now, did your set of belief patterns, what you were 100% sure life was really all about, match exactly with the way your belief patterns work right now?

I am going out on limb here to suggest you do not still view life in quite the same way as you did at sixteen years old. Although at the time, when you were sixteen, you were sure your thoughts and opinions were correct beyond ever questioning them and believed them to be the absolute truth about who you are and the world around you.

OUR TRUTH EVOLVES

Learning to meditate can help a lot here. Later we will get to meditation. Personally I consider this an essential life skill we can all benefit from for multi-layered reasons, not least stress management.

How many times have you gone against some inner feeling of trepidation to nevertheless still forge right ahead with a course of action you kind of knew at some instinctive level did not sit quite comfortably with you?

I have been there and done that. All too often these rationally worked out and procrastinated decisions turn out to be those that are catastrophic in their outcomes.

We will do ourselves a big favour if we opt out of believing every single conscious level thought we have, our constant inner chatter to ourselves; and automatically assuming this must be correct.

After all this is the same inner voice which too often persuades us to maintain the safe status quo to avoid expanding our horizons. It is these inner conversations which lead to us staying put in comfort zones, because it is apparently easier. Truthfully it is never easier to be stuck in a comfort zone, leading to feelings of frustration and lack of control of our destiny. Yet so many of us do manage to convince ourselves to stay right where we are, rather than taking that leap of faith into something new, to see where saying YES takes us.

We will do ourselves the biggest favour by instead developing a habit of trust in our intuition or gut instinct if you like. This bypasses those entire ego driven conscious-level inner conversations we constantly have with ourselves and frees us to usually make the right choice.

Our imagination is one of the most powerful assets we possess. And has practically nothing whatsoever to do with logic or rational thought. It is instead listening to our own intuition 100%.

HAPPINESS IS A CHOICE

Jane felt uncomfortable with compliments or any time a significant date in her life came along, such as her birthday or an anniversary, she felt overwhelmed when receiving gifts and told me she just wanted to run away from the situation. Clearly she had underlying issues, ones which were preventing her from fully enjoying life; and led to her husband and children frustratingly failing to understand why she always reacted in such a way.

Digging down into her childhood revealed she was one of six children, Jane being the middle sister of three girls. As the most responsible of the three sisters she had always looked out for her baby sister, and as there wasn't too much money around, anything Jane received over and above her basic needs being met (occasional foodie treats, gifts or new clothes) she would invariably share with her sisters.

The household was run like a military academy; with six children to feed her parents considered imposed strictness essential for everything to run smoothly. Not surprisingly, Jane felt more than a little starved of love and attention. There was a siege mentality inbred into the children, and Jane would consistently place her personal interests last, to give what meagre things did come her way to her sisters.

Working with Jane over the course of several sessions got her to come to terms with her childhood and see it more in perspective. That her reality today was informed by her experiences growing-up and the guilt led feelings of somehow being unworthy of love or nice things happening for her.

Forgiving her parents finally set her free. Her journey to freedom came through realising her parents were there dealing with the reality of six children, all crammed together along with them in one small house, existing on an extremely limited budget.

As a parent herself, she saw how this must have been understandably stressful at times for them and imposing discipline in the way they had was simply their own coping mechanism, allowing them a sense of feeling a little in control when so often they must not have felt that way at all.

Letting go of the negative feelings and blame through understanding a childhood situation through more informed adult eyes, and more importantly forgiving her parents; who she accepted did the best that they had the capacity to do, finally released Jane from her childhood guilt created emotions. She feel way more at peace when nice things happen to her now and more thoroughly able to enjoy the experience.

As we have already proven with the example of our sixteen-year-old self, our truths continually evolve. Often our inner conversations can stop us right there in our tracks before we can even get properly started; and yet life could be dramatically different if we just simply choose to be happy.

Poor inner conversations about happiness could sound something like this:

1. Well, you know, I need to deal with real everyday life, rather than all this airy-fairy new-age stuff!
2. I am always having to pay those bills, they never seem to grow smaller, am I supposed to feel happy about this?
3. Do not get me started on those stressful trips to the crowded grocery store I must endure every week where the prices are always higher.
4. My life is hard; pretending it isn't will not suddenly make it any better!

Can you or I remain happy yet still deal with all the slings and arrows life may throw at us? Yes, for sure!

Let's go through those four points once more, instead we can choose to observe...

1. Everyday life is where I get to test-out my ability to remain positive.

2. I love having the money to cover my bills and so I must feel happy about being able to pay them.

3. By being mindfully in the moment, I buy-out of the collective group mind wherever I go and whatever I do.

4. Challenges are an opportunity for me to prove to myself just what I am capable of.

Living happy is a choice, and this decision is one any one of us can make at any time. There is a clear path to getting there, one which we are all free to walk.

Being happy does not mean we should adopt a Pollyanna-like attitude to ignore any of life's challenges to pretend nothing is happening. Burying our head in the sand to deceive ourselves everything is fantastically wonderful, when plainly there are issues requiring our attention, is the ultimate inauthentic way to live.

By choosing to be happily optimistic though, no matter what experiences happen along in life, we are more empowered to deal with them, while remaining in personal control of the event. Eventually getting to the point where problems are instead viewed as challenges there to be overcome, rather than seeing them as these horrendously unfair random karmic happenings to lose sleep and worry over.

Happiness is our natural state, and long overdue for us to collectively reclaim as our own.

MIRRORING SMILING

Stand in front of a mirror and look closely at yourself. Pull a face that is comically glum. Now smile warmly at your reflection; observe how this is like an instant face lift which doesn't cost a penny!

Here we are poised at the apex of an excitingly different approach to life and one which is going to unfold to be great fun (frankly, how else?).

Every morning while you are looking in the mirror brushing your teeth or doing your hair and make-up, take a few moments out to look yourself directly in the eyes and smile. Make it a habit to carry on smiling for at least a minute and why not also wish you a happy day at the same time?

Why would you do this?

Well, why not?

This exercise is useful on so many levels; on the one hand here we give ourselves permission to experience a better day. On a deeper level though, looking ourselves directly in the eyes as reflected back through a mirror, does for sure eventually mirror back to us why we habitually go through life running certain programmes.

If being serious and grumpy can unfortunately often become habit-forming for so many, equally so can smiling and being happy become our habit for an empowered life. How about making smiling your new hobby? Waking in the morning, when you first open your eyes, even before you do anything else...smile!

During the day, if you sense stress mounting up to make itself known, and you are starting to feel tense, step away. Take a few moments out and go to the washroom. In privacy smile and keep it up for at least a minute, tell yourself out loud or if you prefer in your mind, that you are happy and will easily cope. Although at first it may well feel like you are acting like you are happy, eventually and surely it will soon arrive at the point where both your subconscious mind and physiology start to believe the messages of happiness they are being consistently subjected to, leading on to becoming your own wonderfully self-fulfilling prophecy.

Every time we practice active smiling not only are we re-programming ourselves to have a different outlook, but we are also creating serotonin and happy endorphins in the chemistry of our brains which act upon our nervous system...making us feel even more happy!

Triggers anchoring us to stay within happiness are useful. Here are twelve triggers, use them every day, buy-into them and watch how your attitude to life changes:

1.   Smile more, it creates serotonin.

2. Find things to laugh about. Read or watch something that hits your laughter buttons; just twenty minutes laughing each day is incredibly de-stressing and helps us stay younger.

3. Are there songs or a genre of music that inspires and lifts your moods? Play them often.

4. Find certain colours uplifting? Wear them often and surround yourself with them.

5. Walking officially lifts our moods, if you feel a little down or lethargic, go and take at least a half-hour walk.

6. Conversation and interaction with positively minded humans can be incredibly uplifting.

7. As is being in love and feeling loved.

8. Spending time with our pets.

9. Enjoy reading? Read inspiring books or stories, expanding our knowledge about something we are interested in makes us feel better.

10. Go smell a rose! Seriously, if you have a garden of your own or a local park, take the time to inhale the heady fragrance of a rose in full bloom, the scent is sure to lift anyone's mood.

11. Volunteering to help others.

12. Crosswords or Sudoku are not only calming, here we have the added benefit of brain-training as well.

It is easy to be enthusiastic when things all seem to be going well for us, how about in the more challenging times though? Those moments when there seems to be a chain reaction of all that challenging stuff happening.

Then is the time to really come alive and show the world empowered enthusiasm consistently achieves goals!

Gratitude Is Everything

It took a rock-climbing accident to open my own eyes to the power of gratitude. In the early days of my recovery simply getting on with the business of regaining my full mobility certainly put my life into focus. The simple act of walking once more became something I appreciated from the bottom of my heart. The same with the sea...

Allow me to explain the sea one!

Part of my self-determined journey to recovery saw me enjoying walking up to my waist in the sea, it was summer and this routine of spending around one hour each day building back my fitness, while feeling the salt water upon my body was an awesome experience And in fact a few decades on from full recovery I still love walking in the sea.

They say that often it takes a life threating or indeed in my case mobility challenging experience to open our eyes to how amazingly wonderful our life genuinely is.

Why wait for such a dramatic event to feel gratitude? There are so many things in life we can feel grateful for right now!

THE WISDOM OF GRATITUDE

Material things bring us temporary pleasure, but it never lasts once the newness wears off.

Far better we choose to feel happy and grateful for being alive regardless of if we have the latest smartwatch or tickets for a month vacationing in Fiji.

Okay, let's roll-out just one more time for posterity the ultimate positive psychology strapline...

Gratitude is the Attitude

I do get that these days this sounds like a bit of cliché, having been used so often by so many and yet the paradox here is that if we do choose to practically place gratitude at the forefront of our day to day living, our life experiences will take on a whole new meaning...

Gratitude for another day absolutely attracts more things to feel grateful for. This alone ought to be motivation enough to focus on what we already have and what appreciation for it might add to our quality of life right now!

Everyone, regardless of their path through life has at least something to appreciate, and these things have often cost nothing to buy. Experiences to feel gratitude for might be down to even the most fundamentally basic of needs being met:

1.   Like clean water to drink.

2. The beauty of a genuine smile given freely; I can personally attest to how this simple act changes lives.

3. Feeling the warming sun shining on our bacs or observing a beautiful cherry tree resplendently in full blossom.

4. Peering out of the window at freshly fallen virgin snow yet to be walked in. As I write this chapter it is an early morning in November in England. The crisp coolness of the night has left both trees and the ground with this glistening diamond-like dusting of frost. This makes me feel thankful to be sat in my warm writing space looking out at it; and anticipating taking a walk out there later to enjoy the sensation of cool cleansing air upon my face.

5. Witnessing a spectacular sunrise or sunset.

6. An interesting conversation shared with a passing someone we met.

7. Having a place to live and a roof over our heads.

8. Those life experiences which have helped shape us into the person we are today.

All the thousand and one things it can become all too easy to sort of take for granted, whereas in fact we ought to view with gratitude from the bottom of our hearts!

We need to feel able to appreciate what we already have. Passionately appreciate who we already are right now. Even though we may well possess the deepest-rooted desire to grow, we need strong foundations to build upon - active gratitude ensures this is the case.

The only way to unlock all the magical things we already have the potential for is to begin by feeling grateful for what we already have and practice active gratitude every day.

ACTIVE GRATITUDE

Get yourself a diary, an old-school paper type, with a page for each day. Let's see how to make the power of gratitude central to our daily routine, until appreciation becomes second nature.

Each morning jot down in your diary three things you feel grateful for. Doesn't matter how small or trivial these may appear to be, and indeed how big or grand they are.

I have been practising this for decades; these are the three gratitude entries I wrote down for this very morning:

1. I am grateful for the cold night which has left glistening frost in its wake.
2. I am grateful for my personal library of books.
3. I am grateful to be aware enough to stay active and fit.

Of course, your entries will likely look entirely different. Active gratitude engenders an appreciation for nature and our own natures. Some past daily entries over the last week have seen me grateful for trees, the gift of sight, freedom to be myself, meditation, the beautiful sky one morning, being a wordsmith and even gratitude for feeling gratitude!

Let active gratitude become second nature and watch the transformation in your life. Make it a habit when first waking up to be genuinely thankful for another day and the opportunities it is surely going to bring.

While you are looking in the mirror in the morning (that early morning bathroom mirror again, for sure this is the most effective moment to programme how your day will unfold) look yourself in the eyes, taking a moment to think of all the things you can feel grateful for. This can be down to the most fundamental of your needs being met, like the fact you even have that mirror to gaze into and a bathroom with instant access to hot and cold water (When so many around the world could only dream of such luxury).

Then write the feelings down in your diary. Your diary then becomes your personal motivational book. If you ever feel challenged by life, you can look back over the daily gratitude entries in your diary, to motivationally remind yourself of who you really are, and how you appreciate life.

Invaluable when we need to keep on keeping on all the way to dealing with challenges and laying them to rest.

Make it fun and enjoy feeling grateful. If you can laugh and smile all the better, positive emotions do carry the message of gratitude infinitely stronger. And the personal energy we put out there into the universe is what makes our life.

We want to be constructing our own life how we desire it rather than events controlling us...gratitude goes a long way to making this real for us.

Building Our Lives

Building a house to stand the test of time begins with firm foundations; it is precisely the same with building a future full of personally inspiring new ideals. Only once the foundations are in place, and in our case this would be having established what we genuinely want from life and how exactly our perfect lifestyle looks, then the real construction can commence. Then arrives the exciting part when we step right ahead to see where this journey will take us!

In our information technology driven world we are easily able to instantly access the answer to virtually any question about practically anything or research the background to whichever person we want to know more about, all right there at our fingertips. Inevitably this can lead us to also sometimes expect these similar kinds of instant results from our lives. For sure we can find ourselves in brilliant new adventures by developing the habit of saying YES to those unexpected opportunities which come our way, however, the truth is that the process of building a completely new lifestyle from the ground up does require dedication and persistence.

Positive changes will never require us slogging away to the detriment of enjoying life. On the contrary, we need to ensure when fulfilling long term goals of any kind, be they improving our health or venturing onto exciting new career paths, that these genuinely improve our quality of day-to-day life.

The only way that our goals stand the best chance of manifesting for us is if we feel happy each day throughout the process of allowing them to happen!

LET LIFE TEACH YOU

If we have consistently done things one way and then suddenly shift our entire intentions this will usually take a little while to show-up in our life.

Think of it like going to university, here though the lecture hall becomes your own life experiences.

You would hardly expect to qualify as a doctor in three months, becoming proficient at taking control of your own life is precisely the same. Mastery comes through experience. Learning opportunities will be encountered. You are educating yourself and your ongoing life is the lecturer.

Every time we become aware of and then leave behind any deeply entrenched mindset, one we have for far too long bought-into that might have limited our ideal lifestyle from existing; we are placing ourselves so much closer to this same ideal lifestyle's permanence.

ACCEPT THE GIFT

What if a person you are loosely acquainted with, from the outer edge of your extended circle of friends totally out of the blue offered you an all-expenses paid holiday of your choice? All you needed to do was pick the destination and turn up at the airport on the day. How would you react?

How about a distant second cousin randomly deciding to gift you a new car? What then?

Moving closer to home, how do you feel if your temporarily unemployed friend insists that he wants to stand his round of drinks at the bar or you receive an unexpectedly generous birthday present from an elderly relative who relies only on her pension to live?

With the law of universal energy taken into consideration there really can be only one response.

Smile as you graciously accept the gift and be happy for the generosity of the perpetrator, for surely their actions in due course are about to bring about many good happenings into their own life. To react in any other way we are treating ourselves like we are somehow unworthy of good things happening.

We always deserve good things happening in our lives. Irrespective of what we may have always thought to the contrary. It is our birth right to deserve to feel good...to be happy!

We need to allow for the good flow of energy. Any freely offered gift needs to be accepted with peace and grace. This is our role in the transaction.

And this can equally take the form of the gift of someone giving of their time, listening to us rather than doing the talking. This opportunity also must be cheerfully accepted and with due gratitude. Any other course of action would be interrupting the giver's personal energetic flow of attracting good things via the actions of their own energy and you or I certainly don't have the right to do any such a thing!

Always feel comfortable with accepting a freely offered gift and develop the habit of feeling infinitely happy for the giver's generosity. Knowing that for sure it will boomerang straight back into their life at some point and probably soon.

Why not also get into the habit of freely giving kindness to others for creating mini miracles in your own life?

Feel Instant Confidence

The way we present our physiology to the world reveals precisely how we view ourselves. And anyone who understands even the fundamentals of body language will be able to pick up on these signals.

Through our posture we lock-in how we feel, this indicates our current emotional state and level of self-esteem. And yet we can make the choice to transform all this in a moment and the effects are immediate!

This takes us far beyond basic body language, directly into using our own physiology to create the moods we want to experience and powerfully feeling in control.

We have an amazing lever at our disposal here and it really is practically so simple that you could well initially have difficulty in accepting it can make such a radical difference in your life. It does!

This is one of the most popular subjects I cover in my talks, once my audiences get what a radical transformation our physiology can make in how they feel and are perceived by the world. Typically, at my events I demonstrate three models of physiological behaviour - starting with a political candidate looking to be elected, next a supermodel strutting her stuff down the catwalk and conclude with a dishonest salesperson. These comedic representations of physiological archltypes serve to illustrate the point in a way which usually stays with my audiences and demonstrates I am quite happy to look silly in the name of our greater understanding!

Applying your physiology to work for you through transforming your happiness, confidence and integrity is 100% experiential. Once you have put this into practice for yourself, then you will get how powerfully this works.

SMILE MORE

Release that serotonin and you start to feel better almost immediately, and others will gravitate towards you more. Remember this simple game-changing trick; smiling makes anything we need to deal with seem a little easier.

Genuine laughter is free and changes moods in a moment.

LOOK UP

If we are feeling down we also tend to walk around looking down at the ground.

Want to feel instantly better? Look up! What could be simpler?

Rather than staring down at the ground or a mobile phone screen while walking or indeed sitting, instead look upwards towards the horizon. Pay attention to the architecture way up there at the top of buildings, see those things higher up in the landscape so many miss through waking around looking at their own feet. Raise your gaze to look at trees, birds in flight and the pattern of clouds in the sky. Develop this habit to feel more positively happy (but still be sure to look where you are walking!).

OPEN GESTURES

Any gesture where we fold our arms across our body is protective (unless we feel cold or in pain when we will fold our arms to keep heat in or hug ourselves for comfort).

The same with habitually having hands stuck in our pockets, this is also protective, and others will intuitively pick up on this signal. We can kick this self-limitation into touch instantly to raise our internal confidence barometer! I have not folded my arms for over two decades (seriously).

By avoiding folding our arms and keeping hands out of pockets, once we get over the strangeness of this new habit, we do genuinely start to feel far more confident and personally empowered.

POSTURE

How we stand affects the way we feel.

Take the time to observe a successful person you admire as they interact out there in the big wide world.

How do they stand and walk?

How is it different from your posture and walk?

Chances are, whatever their physical size, they stand up straight and walk tall – meaning their posture is upright, shoulders back as they squarely look the world in the eyes. Mirroring this walking success story to adjust your own stance and walk will pay instant dividends in terms of the way it makes you feel so powerfully more confident!

SEATED POSTURE

At home feel free to loll away in your favourite chair. In the workplace or when attending business meetings we come across as far more engaged if our posture is upright (but not rigid) with our head facing in the general direction of whoever is doing the talking.

I know that might seem almost too obvious, that we need to look at the person talking, believe me I have been in front of enough audiences over the decades to easily observe who is genuinely engaged in what I am saying and those who are more interested in what they might grab for lunch in the intermission!

Paying attention means we are mindfully engaged right there in the moment; others will notice and respect our opinion far more. We will also tend to remember what was being said, which is always useful.

SHAKING HANDS

We will have all met those bone-crushers who shake hands like they are taking part in some kind of iron man style power contest. We also know this makes them look anything but powerful; instead they come across as immature.

At the other end of the scale we will have experienced those who shake hands like a damp dishcloth, while failing to make any eye contact.

The happy balance here is a firm handshake, while making eye contact and then let go. We come across as business-like and confident, happily re-enforcing us feeling more business-like and confident.

FACE TOUCHING

Typical gestures of a liar are nose, mouth or eye scratching, oh and ear rubbing (their own, not yours!) and also shifting around within their stood or seated position. If we witness at least a few of these micro-gestures from someone, the chances are they are being economical with the truth.

If you find yourself often using these gestures, improve your choice of words to communicate with more integrity to get your opinions listened to and taken seriously.

Anyone who consciously avoids face touching gestures or shifting around when talking will find themselves quite automatically communicating in an entirely different way, with some real integrity.

PHYSIOLOGY SUMMARY

Taking on board these physiological gifts for yourself is such an easy and instant way to transform your life as you apply them. The positive results we get are always the most convincing validation of anything we adopt which is new.

Combining positive physiology with the right mindset awakens our inner genius...

Astrological Harmony

One of the first leftfield subjects I studied over three decades ago was astrology. This is in the days before we could just type a date of birth into a search engine to freely obtain a birth chart. I learned the old school way to cast a chart and interpret the results.

Our basic Sun Sign can act as a kind of template to discover ways of living in greater happiness and wellbeing. Obviously our moon and ascendant impact upon us greatly, but having said that, there are traits remaining common to most born under a particular Sun Sign.

ARIES

Date - 21 March to 20 April.

Ruling - Planet Mars.

Colours - Aries people might notice subtle differences in their health and well-being by wearing or surrounding themselves with particularly red or any other bright fiery colours. Red plays to the more aggressive side of the nature of the Aries person and others may find they are coming across a bit full-on. From the Aries point of view the art is in being able to wear the colour red without it dominating them or bringing out an overly aggressive side.

Crystal - Red Jasper for costume jewellery or uncut pieces for around the home.

Gem - Ruby for jewellery.

Metal - Iron in the general environment.

Flower - Honeysuckle

Lucky Number - 9

Foods - Red onions, tomatoes and beetroot, avoid too highly spiced food.

Essential Oil – Cinnamon.

Health - The ruling planet of Aries is Mars, which governs the head. Avoid the type of stress which might lead to migraines and ensure enough liquid is consumed to avoid dehydration. Aries people need to be especially vigilant to take care of their head and related parts of their body.

Careers - Aries people generally enjoy being in charge, any occupation that lets them be a leader is ideal for them. As long as there is someone to take care of the small details, then the Aries person can lead well from the front. Often inspirational and rarely lacking friends, they are highly driven and if they positively channel their aggression into their career, the Aries person will reach the top.

Personality Traits - Can be impulsive, highly positive and inspirational, energetic, enthusiastic, sometimes a little vain, good leaders, ambitious, competitive, confident and maybe a little too trusting sometimes leading to hurt feelings. Aries are people persons and usually good fun to be around.

TAURUS

Date - 21 April to 21 May

Ruling Planet – Venus.

Colours - Taurus people might well notice subtle differences in their health and well-being by wearing or surrounding themselves with particularly pink or pale blue, also deep green. Pink is the ideal colour for both sexes if they are Taurean; worn it brings out the best side in their nature or in their surroundings helps them to feel at peace

Crystal - Rose Quartz for costume or fine jewellery and although Pink Kunzite is classed as the Gemstone for Taurus, really pink Rose Quartz suits them like no other crystal. Rough, uncut Rose Quartz is wonderful to place around their environment.

Gemstone - Pink Kunzite for fine jewellery.

Metal - Copper in jewellery or in their home-space.

Flower – Rose.

Lucky Number - 6

Foods - Beans, spinach, melon, apples, apricots and almonds, Taurus people would be definitely better to avoid any type of red meat for the ease of their digestive system.

Essential Oil - Rose, calms like no other oil for the Taurean and rather beautiful for anyone actually!

Health - The ruling planet of Taurus is Venus, which governs the throat. Avoid too much shouting or saying harsh words. Taurus people need to be especially careful to take care of their throats and associated parts of the body.

Careers - Taurus people are known to be highly creative and artistic. They can also make good writers. Jobs dealing with financial matters are also ideal for Taureans. The Taurean employee is usually conscientious and they work well as team leaders, as long as they are recognized for their abilities.

Personality Traits - The Taurus person is usually practical, trustworthy and patient. The Taurean will often have a love of luxury and appreciation for the finer things in life. They can be determined and extremely strong willed; liking things to be done their way, which others will either find harmonious or not...if listened to though the Taurean is more often than not right. Taurus people will usually have a definite plan for life, even going so far as writing out lists of things they wish to achieve or the ideal traits in a potential partner.

GEMINI

Date - 22 May to 21 June

Ruling Planet – Mercury.

Colour - Gemini people may notice subtle differences in their health and well-being by wearing or surrounding themselves with particularly pale grey, silver or silver grey. The Gemini person needs to surround themselves with silver if possible, wear it, have it in the environment and if a driver, choose a car this colour.

Crystal - Grey Agate for costume or fashion jewellery.

Gemstone - Silver Topaz for fine jewellery.

Metal - Silver for any kind of jewellery or fashion accessory.

Flower - Lily-of-the-Valley.

Lucky Number - 5

Foods - Carrots, all kinds of nuts, wheat bread and parsley. Homemade bread is perfect for the Gemini, as are soups containing carrots.

Essential Oils - Clary Sage.

Health - The ruling planet of Gemini is Mercury, which governs the nervous system. Avoid getting stressed out and the Gemini might like to consider taking up a martial art, as this would be especially beneficial to them. Gemini people need to take be especially vigilant to take care of their nervous system and associated parts of their body.

Careers - Gemini people are highly versatile and as such can succeed in many professions including journalism, travel writer, sales or as some kind of instructor; in fact any job that allows them to keep moving and avoid getting bored by doing the same thing day in day out. Routine will never work for a Gemini and often during their life they will have many careers to excel in, and they often will excel as well.

Personality Traits - Can be charming and witty. Gemini people are born with an innate love of talking and debating. Frequently subject to quick changes of mood that others can sometimes have difficulty in keeping up with. Usually enjoys travelling and exploring new places. Gemini people are a bit of a law unto themselves, but are generally hugely entertaining to have as friends.

CANCER

Date - 22 June to 23 July

Ruling Planet - The Moon

Colour - Cancer people might well notice subtle differences in their health and well-being by wearing or surrounding themselves with particularly pearly white and accessorize with emerald green. Cancerians would benefit from avoiding drab, dark colours; they need to wear basically the shades associated with the moon or at least surround themselves with these colours in their décor.

Crystal - Moonstone for jewellery, preferably mounted in silver.

Gemstone - Moonstone

Metal - Silver for jewellery and fashion accessories.

Flower - Wild flowers in a meadow.

Lucky Number - 2

Foods - All kinds of green leafy salads, watermelon and lettuce. Raw food works especially well for the Cancerians, salad is the perfect choice.

Essential oil - Chamomile

Health - The ruling planet of Cancer is the Moon, which governs the chest (plus emotions). It is essential for the Cancer person to avoid people or situations where they are likely to be upset or disrespected. Cancer people need to take be especially careful to look after the emotional side of their life and take care with their cardiovascular health.

Careers - Cancer people prefer to work in a career which deals with helping the public or in the caring professions. They make popular and charismatic primary school teachers. Cancerians care about others, any job that allows them to utilize this side of themselves will work well for them. Often artistic, the Cancerian likes the stability of a given wage, so perhaps their artistic side can be developed more as a hobby, rather than living as the archetypal struggling artist.

Personality Traits - The Cancer person is usually sensitive, kind and emotional. They enjoy their home life and will work on it being smooth and free from arguments. If their home is stable and welcoming Cancer people then do enjoy to travel and explore the World, as long as they know they have somewhere safe to come home to then they are open to all manner of global adventures. Good with money usually and exercise extra caution when dealing with financial speculation. Don't ask your Cancerian acquaintance for a loan, as refusal can often offend and they more than likely will say no. Their moods can change with the phases of the Moon. Did I say moody? Well sometimes perhaps a little bit, but they can be forgiven that for all their other crazy fun-to-be-around qualities.

LEO

Date - 24 July to 23 August

Ruling Planet - The Sun

Colour - Leo people might notice subtle differences in their health and well-being by wearing or surrounding themselves with particularly golden yellow and royal purple. Leos are the royalty of all the sun signs, wearing gold and deep purple will definitely have the feel-good factor for them.

Crystal - Gold Tiger-eye for all types of jewellery, mounted in gold.

Gemstone - Amber in fine jewellery, mounted with the finest quality of gold.

Metal - Gold, naturally what else?

Flower - Sunflower

Lucky Number - 1

Foods - Citrus foods, honey, dates and raisins, in fact all sun-dried fruits.

Essential Oil - Orange

Health - The ruling planet of Leo is the Sun, which governs the heart. Leo people need to feel loved, especially by their own self. Avoiding an overly rich diet is essential and they need to take be especially careful to take care their heart and associated parts of their body.

Careers - Leo people excel at any profession when they feel that they are appreciated and receive recognition for what they do. Most Leo people enjoy being a little adored every now and again. The Leo person would make a good front person for any business, be it receptionist or front of house; anything that allows their warm, friendly personality to shine. Many great television hosts are Leo, there is something truly lovable about a happy Leo and the warmth they project to everyone at every level of life.

Personality Traits - If they are well balanced their over-riding trait will be pride, which can work either way for the Leo person as others will either adore them for it or consider them perhaps a little arrogant. Confident, warm and usually generous by nature the Leo does rarely lack friends. Enjoys an audience and has a great inbuilt sense of showmanship. Fond of good living and appreciates luxury. A Leo has a definite sense of their own worth and expects this to be recognized by others as well

VIRGO

Date - 24 August to 23 September

Ruling Planet - Mercury

Colour - Virgo people might well notice subtle differences in their health and well-being by wearing or surrounding themselves with particularly white, silver or jade green. White, cream or pale silver when worn or used in interior design will help the Virgo person to feel more themselves.

Crystal - Carnelian for all kinds of jewellery.

Gemstone - Jade for particularly items in the home such as statues or icons.

Metal - Platinum for jewellery.

Flower - Nut bearing trees.

Lucky Number - 5

Foods - Carrots, oatmeal, parsley and all kinds of nuts. Porridge with almonds is an excellent choice for breakfast. Carrot-sticks or carrot soups and avoidance of too spicy food.

Essential Oils - Peppermint

Health - The ruling planet of Virgo is Mercury, which governs the whole digestive system. The need to remain calm is essential for Virgo people. Care needs to be taken to be sure not to over-tax their finely balanced digestive system and avoiding junk food is essential.

Careers - Virgo people are great at organizing and it has been said they would be better to work in a profession that allows them to use these skills in their job such as accountancy and book-keeping. The Virgo person does paradoxically have another alternative side to them and many high-profile people in the entertainment industry are in fact Virgos such as the late Freddie Mercury and Michael Jackson, so perhaps if they have a talent in that area they need to concentrate on nurturing it and go on to become the next great actor, singer or comedian.

Personality Traits - By nature analytical and meticulous; yet they can also be gregarious given the right circumstances. There is a common misconception that a Virgo person is like a walking computer...they do in fact generally have a great sense of fun and humour; and can quite enjoy the glare of the spotlight for short periods of time, as long as it is on their terms...perhaps to retreat from the world every once in a while to recharge their batteries. Likes to have a set routine and plenty of advanced warning about change.

LIBRA

Date - 24 September to 23 October

Ruling Planet - Venus

Colour - Libran people may notice subtle differences in their health and well-being by wearing or surrounding themselves with particularly pale blue and pink, also green. The combination of pale blue and green in their décor will be calming to the Libran person.

Crystal - Green Aventurine for fashion or costume jewellery.

Gemstone - Malachite as jewellery, especially when mounted in copper.

Metal - Copper for jewellery and items around the home.

Flower - Bluebells

Lucky Number - 6

Foods - Cereals, almonds, beans and dried fruits. Avoiding red meat is certainly believed to benefit their health.

Essential Oil - Geranium

Health - The ruling planet of Libra is Venus, which governs the kidneys. Watching their diet is almost mandatory for the Libran as overburdening their body with too much poor-quality foodstuff can lead to potential health challenges to be overcome. The purer their diet, the better their potential for amazing positive health.

Careers - Libran people have a natural affinity with money and balance sheets, accountancy and bookkeeping would work well. With their usual exquisite taste they also have an inbuilt appreciation of art and good design, therefore working in galleries or as a designer would be good professions, perhaps as a retailer selling fine goods. The caring professions or teaching can also be attractive options for the Libran.

Personality Traits - Typically possessing good taste, inbuilt diplomacy and the ability to look at situations in a completely detached way. Generally easy going in nature and pleasant people to be around; often blessed with a charismatic smile. Librans find harshness and disharmony highly distasteful; they will cut out of their life anyone who creates that kind of chaos and to the Libran they will simply cease to exist. Good judges of character.

SCORPIO

Date - 24 October to 22 November

Ruling Planet - Pluto

Colour - Scorpio people might notice subtle differences in their health and well-being by wearing or surrounding themselves with particularly deep blue, purple and black. Mysterious by nature, dark colours suit the Scorpio person perfectly and you will sometimes even find they have a penchant for wearing dark glasses, all of which harmonizes brilliantly with their sun sign nature.

Crystal - Bloodstone in all kinds of jewellery.

Gemstone - Jet, traditionally used in mourning jewellery, today it is still available in some wonderfully gothic one-off jewellery pieces and these would suit the Scorpio person perfectly.

Metal - Steel to wear or used in interior design. Carbon steel is sometimes fashioned into jewellery.

Flower - All dark maroon flowers, especially Roses.

Lucky Number - 10 and paradoxically also 0

Foods - Rye breads, highly spicy dishes, dates. The Scorpio thrives on an exotic diet many other sun signs would find over-powerfully spicy. Indian, Moroccan and Mexican cuisine are attractive options.

Essential Oil - Myrrh

Health - The ruling planet of Scorpio is Pluto, which governs the reproductive system. Scorpio people need to take be especially vigilant in taking care of this and associated parts of their body.

Career - Scorpio people excel in professions that allow them to use their powerful mind. They enjoy being able to troubleshoot and solve problems. The Scorpio person would make a good detective, analytical chemist, scientist or indeed any career that allows them to investigate and uncover the truth. The Scorpio writer will thrill their readers with the complexity of their stories or if they are an artist will thrive at shocking the establishment by pushing boundaries within their chosen area of artistic endeavour.

Personality Traits - The Scorpio is definitely difficult to ignore – powerful minds and the ability to see through deception. Can sometimes come across as a bit intense and serious, however, a happy Scorpio is wonderful company and s entertaining. Scorpios enjoy mysteries and understanding what motivates people. Can like to keep things to themselves until they feel ready to share and for sure, will ensure one way or another that events play out the way they planned them and you can be equally sure that they will have certainly made a plan!

SAGITTARIUS

Date - 23 November to 21 December

Ruling Planet - Jupiter

Colour - Sagittarius people might well notice subtle differences in their health and well-being by wearing or surrounding themselves with particularly turquoise or bright yellow. Wearing turquoise or nice sunny yellow brings out the best in the Sagittarius person and certainly goes some way to ensuring a sunny disposition.

Crystal - Blue Howlite, this looks a lot like real turquoise and is an ideal low-cost option for fashion or costume jewellery.

Gemstone - Turquoise is a wonderful gem for the Sagittarius person to wear.

Metal - Tin

Flower - Dandelion

Lucky Number - 3

Foods - Berries, grapes, nuts and wheat cereals.

Essential Oil - lemon

Health - The ruling planet of Sagittarius is Jupiter, which governs the hips and upper legs. Keeping fit is essential for Sagittarius people and they need to take be especially careful to take care to remain mobile and in good physical shape.

Careers - Sagittarius people usually adore animals and sometimes feel the need to work with them in some capacity. They also enjoy pushing back the boundaries within their chosen career and can find routine extremely boring. They have an easy understanding of machinery and engineering, a profession that allows them to exploit this will work well for them. Being a responsible manager, sat behind a desk all day, will not really work well for the Sagittarius person.

Personality Traits - Energetic approach to life and enthusiastic. Often keen on sport or competitive games. Honest with their opinions, which some can find the bluntness with the way their truths are expressed offensive, although it is never usually their intention to upset anyone and often the Sagittarius person cannot understand what they did to offend. Having said that they are usually happy and fun to be with, people generally like Sagittarians and seek out their company.

CAPRICORN

Date - 22 December to 20 January

Ruling Planet - Saturn

Colour - Capricorn people may notice subtle differences in their health and well-being by wearing or surrounding themselves with particularly dark green or blue. Paradoxically bringing some bright colours into their environment such as yellow can be lifting to the spirit of a Capricorn person.

Crystal - Obsidian Snowflake for fashion or costume jewellery.

Gemstone - Diamond

Metal - Lead

Flower - Pansies

Lucky Number - 8

Foods - Broccoli, spinach, celery and potatoes.

Essential Oil - Patchouli

Health - The ruling planet of Capricorn is Saturn, which governs the knees and shins. Capricorn people need to take be especially careful to take care of this part of their body.

Careers - Capricorn people are usually ambitious, so need to work in a profession where there are opportunities for advancement and promotion. They do enjoy working with plants and the soil but could be equally at home in an office or factory, just as long as they can feel they are getting somewhere and will ultimately be promoted. Generally a Capricorn is respected in the workplace and their opinion valued and sought.

Personality Traits - Patient and able to concentrate on the task in hand all the way to completion, before moving on. Capricorn people are usually more serious when they are younger and become more relaxed as they mature. Careful with financial dealings and speculation. Happy to patiently bide their time to reach their goals; which they usually achieve. If you make a friend of a Capricorn and never deceive or offend them, you most definitely have a friend for life.

AQUARIUS

Date - 21 January to 19 February

Ruling Planet - Uranus

Colour - Aquarius people could notice subtle differences in their health and well-being by wearing or surrounding themselves with particularly electric blue, ocean green and purple. Aquarians would definitely benefit from wearing at least one of those colours or with their usual abstract approach to life, perhaps all at the same time! Oceanic colours in their environment will be calming.

Crystal Rock Crystal/Clear Quartz - in all kinds of jewellery and as crystals to have around the home.

Gemstone - Aquamarine mounted in platinum as fine jewellery.

Metal - Platinum

Flower - Orchid and Foxglove.

Lucky Number - 4

Foods - Spinach, all types of fruit. Aquarius people would be better to be vegetarian.

Essential Oil - Lavender

Health - The ruling planet of Aquarius is Uranus, which governs the ankles. Aquarius people need to take be especially careful to take care of this part of their body.

Careers - Aquarius people are natural innovators and prefer to work in jobs that allow them to use their often off-the-wall originality, with some freedom to express their visionary individuality. They are sometimes drawn to the caring professions and are able to help others, while remaining realistic about those they are helping. Wonderfully abstract, so careers where this can be utilized suit the Aquarian best.

Personality Traits - Friendly, usually independent and non-judgmental. Often unpredictable, unconventional and abstract; and usually hugely entertaining company. The Aquarian lives by their own rules and doesn't care much for the conventions of society. Enjoys communicating and usually has a great sense of humour.

PISCES

Date - 20 February to 20 March

Ruling Planet - Neptune

Colour - Pisces people may well notice subtle differences in their health and well-being by wearing or surrounding themselves with particularly sea green, aqua blue and white. Dark colours will feel oppressive to the Piscean.

Crystal - Amethyst in any kind of jewellery and pieces of this crystal around the home.

Gemstone - Gem quality Amethyst for fine jewellery, preferably mounted in silver or platinum.

Metal - Tin

Flower Water - Lily

Lucky Number - 7

Foods - Salad, mushroom, fruit salad, fruit juice.

Essential Oil - Ylang Ylang

Health - the ruling planet of Pisces is Neptune, which governs the feet. Pisces people need to take be especially careful to take care of this part of their body.

Careers - Pisces people usually shy away from the type of jobs that require routine and a lot of discipline, having said that they can be good at studying and enjoy educating others; so teaching, professorship and story-telling harmonize well for the Pisces person. Make especially good writers, with their strong imaginations; also psychology and counselling are attractive to the Piscean and would work well.

Personality Traits - Sensitive, emotional and generally sympathetic. Often intuitive, people tend to tell them their problems, knowing they can be trusted. Can be a little vague on details and avoids confrontations if at all possible. Sometimes can be a little secretive, they can also live in their imagination, although a happy Piscean will less feel the need to do this.

AFTERWORD

On a personal note, I am a Piscean with Leo Moon and Virgo Ascendant; helping others is my passion. Helping others, is for me living in harmony with the reason I was born onto this planet. It feels right and for all of us alike, if it feels right deep inside, then it is! If you can find out your sun, moon and ascendant, look at them as well to combine the suggested recommendations for complete harmony with the essence of you.

Helpful Thoughts

What we consistently think about affects firstly our own self-image and consequently how we are then perceived by others. Our thoughts (and words) also directly influence our actual physical wellbeing and mental health.

The cells of your body and mind, every single moment of every single day, are bombarded with thoughts and more crucially the emotions felt behind those thoughts. We have the thoughts of ourselves and like it or not, also the thoughts of those around us. And our bodies and minds will listen to these messages and words it receives loud and clear, reacting accordingly regardless of our conscious awareness of it.

We create our personal version of reality through thoughts. What we think, feel, and say is played forward as the reality of our life.

Yet if we care to listen to those words of others when they voice opinions about us to our face, to a greater or lesser degree these validations of how they see us or the kind of life we ought to be leading, can affect our inner and outer well-being. All depending quite literally upon how much credence we give to their point of view!

Our health, happiness and financial reality are reactions to the messages we are constantly sending out about ourselves and receiving from others.

For sure this can all be different though...radically different. That word **choice** comes into play once more.

Throughout much of this book my goal is specifically aimed at breaking down any of your unconscious self-limitation habits - to instead place you right there in the pole position of deciding where your life goes.

It seems almost too obvious to state that feeling good about YOU is vital for happiness and living beyond any possible self-imposed limitation! Yet many of us do run programmes forward into our lives which achieve anything but that desired outcome.

Think of people you know. Do those who moan and complain all the time come across as brilliantly happy examples of humanity?

Or the professional cynic, expletively going through life mocking others and exhibiting sarcasm, do they seem full of joy?

Are those who fixate on illness usually healthy?

At the other end of the scale, how about those teachers at high-school who always seemed to have a ready smile and were encouragingly inclusive with the pupils in their class, perhaps you met at least one of these educational gems on your journey through school? These teachers rarely had to discipline students as they were too engaged with learning, and everyone felt better for attending their lessons.

Or how about the neighbour who is genuinely interested in what we have to say, never gossips, and laughs along with our jokes, don't you feel good for passing a few moments with them? These guys are happy people, sure they have their share of issues like all of us, yet they choose to face the day with a smile and pleasant words.

FOCUSSING AND ACTING ON WHAT WE WANT

If I would love to be a scratch golfer, sitting there each day chanting affirmations *"I am grateful to be a scratch golfer"* yet taking absolutely no personal action myself to achieve this goal will never automatically make me go around the course in par. How I can make it work though is if I take the time to study and carefully mirror the mindset of a professional golfer I admire. Then as perfectly as I am able, replicate their playing techniques to make it all real. I incrementally increase the chances I will genuinely soon enjoy being that scratch golfer!

The subconscious mind acts like a data storage file for all our experiences.

And we constantly programme our subconscious through our consistent thoughts, words and actions. We are our own self-fulfilling idea of exactly how we should look and shape of the future life experiences we will have. And every one of us constantly does this completely regardless of whether we are ever aware of the fact.

YET WE HAVE A CHOICE

Our mindset is 100% in our own hands. We truly can think whatever we choose...

Rather usefully our freedom of choice means that we can go right ahead this very moment to mould our own life for ourselves, choose how we learn from our experiences. Reclaiming our personal power to take charge of shaping our future destiny by simply choosing exactly what we centre our conscious thoughts on.

It is all too easy to lose track of our own motivations, personal standards and authentic self, if we pay too much attention to the constant stream of words coming our way from even well-meaning family and friends, never mind about those toxic people we all encounter from time to time! The next chapter will help...

(Dis)Comfort Zones

Public speaking had already become second nature to me, I felt (and still do) a buzz of excitement stood before an audience to communicate. This will always be an inherently two-way communication. I know my story inside out; I prefer hear yours I can help you more effectively. I often get asked if I feel nervous before giving a talk. Never, I love what I do and standing in front of an audience open to learning life-transforming techniques is an amazingly life-affirming experience.

I never work from scripts. I trust when I get up I will automatically have the words to impart the points I wish to cover; and because of this every event sees me adapting my subject matter once I begin to sense what will work best for this particular audience. As with my writing, I feel my role as a public speaker is to mainly get out of my own way to allow the relevant information to reach my readers and audience through me.

Poetry was an altogether different proposition!

The prospect of laying myself creatively on the line, publicly sharing my poetry for the first time led me to question my sanity more than once as the date of the evening literary festival approached. I felt compelled to go ahead regardless though, if only to walk the talk once again and live the message I have been sharing with others for years about the leaving of comfort zones.

As I arrived at the venue on the night in question the organiser came to see me backstage and asked me for a favour. Having attended one of my Holistic Living Events, he already knew how I function in front of an audience; he asked if I might mentor two nervous first-time performance poets and let them share the stage with me, then they would feel more at ease. He assumed, as a regular on stage I knew what I was doing and equally assumed that I must have performed poetry many times before. All my own concerns forgotten, of course I said YES to his request.

And us three went on stage together that night, standing next to one another at microphones, with me there in the middle lending them an extra sense of security. I introduced us all, performed a poem, and led my new friends through their own performances, each of us taking turns to share our creative endeavours. It was brilliant fun and for the hour we had been allotted I believe we managed to entertain our audience. Well they applauded when we reached the end and before that laughed at the right moments, so chances are they enjoyed our poetic tales.

Ironically the organiser did me a great favour that night without knowing it. He placed me straight into a mindset I felt 100% comfortable with. Mentoring others; helping them to find the inner confidence to leave their comfort zones, resulted in me not even considering mine anymore. After all mentoring is my stock-in-trade, it is what I do! My own misgiving completely forgotten, out I went personally feeling as if I had been performing poetry for years and that is exactly how everyone perceived me.

Mindset is everything and the apparent limitation of a comfort zone might well turn out to have been a mirage after all, once we choose to do something awesome to embrace a slightly scary new experience.

Thought patterns get hard-wired into the neural pathways in our brains. The more we practise doing something the better we get. Yet, unfortunately not all these neural pathways work in our best interests. They become a self-limiting way of life and usually it takes a wake-up call to transform away from these patterns and form a new neural pathway or paradigm.

THE THIRD THOUGHT

For many people their thought processes, those inner conversation going on through their conscious minds, go something along these lines:

THOUGHT ONE A brilliantly original idea or concept seemingly appears out of nowhere. Maybe it is in their mind as they awaken one morning; perhaps observing something in passing opens their eyes to a hitherto unseen opportunity or an overheard conversation suddenly inspires them to see the world in an entirely new way. Naturally they feel engaged and excited at this point.

THOUGHT TWO Now to do something about this amazing inspiration! For a short while their mind works overtime on different positive ways this idea can happen for real. Practically getting from where, what at the moment is the idea, carrying on all the way through to its magnificent realization, consumes their attention full-time.

THOUGHT THREE They gradually begin having an inner conversation of limitation. Helping them find some valid (and poor) excuses for inaction. Next they persuade themselves how it would all be far more sensible to not really have this happen anyway. Their new excuses convince them that this was all a terrible idea after all. Far better to stay put right there in their comfort zone (trapped) because this is always the easier option.

We have all just witnessed a comfort zone in action. Sadly, this mindset single-handedly stops more potential winners from achieving their goals than anything else. How many incredibly pioneering inventions or life changing innovations have been lost to comfort zone self-limitation we will never know.

It bears repeating that repetition creates habits; this fact is invaluable when opting to move our life forward. The more we do something new the more we lock-it into ourselves until it gradually becomes second nature to act or think within this new paradigm.

It is precisely the same with those old, entrenched comfort zones – we hold so tightly onto them precisely because we have always thought or done things that way. And yet we always possessed the freedom to live beyond comfort zones; by-passing all those inner conversations we run through our minds, those self-justifying excuses for inaction.

Only possessing knowledge of the existence of these inner conversations of limitation goes a long way towards reducing their power over us.

Through this awareness we can recognise them for what they are when faced with any moments of decision making and choose to buy-out of running those old programmes once and for all.

LOVING TO PAY TAX

Back in the early days of The Strawberry Crystal a few decades ago, each year I would take myself off to my accountant as it came the designated time to file my annual accounts, and each time for sure I dreaded being informed the amount of tax I found myself burdened with needing to pay for that year. It never grew smaller; in my mind it seemed to me I was working hard in my business to fund the tax office and keep all those guys employed. Dave, my accountant would usually shrug his shoulders and remind me to pay my tax before the due date.

One particular year along came that dreaded tax-time again, only for me to discover Dave had promptly taken early retirement due to poor health. I needed to find a new accountant and fast!

A recommendation led me to Amanda; recently having left one the big accountancy firms to set up in practice for herself. Her advert tagline went something along the lines of 'Innovating New Approaches To Accountancy'. I liked the sound of this and duly made an appointment.

Bringing along my accounts files for Amanda to look over, during the meeting I mentioned my usual grievance about how each year since I started in business I needed to pay more tax and how I felt I was working for the government.

She looked over her glasses across the desk at me. *"Dean, I love having to pay more tax each year, this means I must be becoming more successful each year and if I am earning a higher percentage of profits annually then I have to be doing things right. My taxable income increasing year in year out is really what motivates me, as I know my turnover is heading in the right direction!"*

Okay, this one took a few moments to sink-in. I suppose I must have looked a little shocked as I sat there for at least a minute staring at her temporarily speechless.

In one short statement Amanda had managed to entirely transform my belief patterns regarding paying tax. She gifted me a new paradigm.

Before this my mindset and thoughts had been focused entirely on the 35% (or whatever it literally was at the time) of anything I earned needing to be given to the government in tax and increasingly resenting when each year this amount grew. From that moment on I loved paying my tax, especially if it turned out to be significantly higher than the previous tax year. I knew if this happened I must have equally significantly increased my profits that year.

A friend recently stated that if he worked overtime at the weekend he would have to pay 40% in tax on everything he earned. I suggested he would be wiser to look at this as earning 60% more than if he hadn't done the overtime. Given his grumpy *"I suppose so"* response I am not sure he is quite ready yet to buy-into my proffered different way of looking at his reality.

How we chose to look at life ensures the experience we will have in that same life.

A comfort zone is much like an old favourite jacket, it's a little shabby and doesn't look too cool these days, yet carries on being worn because it feels comfortable.

Although many of us do for sure initially have every intention of carrying through with a plan or working towards fulfilling a long-held goal, unfortunately for the majority it does not quite end up playing out like that. They end up buying into Third Thought excuse making instead...

EXCUSES WON'T CUT IT ANYMORE

Some hold onto the excuse "It's just my karma" to validate their reasons for remaining static, they feel this is a good enough reason to stay exactly where they are. To be blunt, this is a poor excuse for inaction.

And my word is the ever so many more awful excuses for inaction!

Proclamations along the lines of:

- "Oh well, you know nobody in my family ever achieved much so I guess I'm just going to accept that I won't either"

- "I tried further education after I left school as a teenager and when it didn't work-out I felt like a failure, I'm never going to study anything new again"
- "It's not my fault I wake up every day lacking in any energy and motivation, it's just my genes"
- And we also have the classic one "I'm too young, old, short, tall, underqualified, overqualified, beautiful, ugly, unconventional, shy (delete as appropriate)!"

Every single one of these frankly garbage excuses need to now be thrown right into the trash where they belong!

Before we leave excuses, I must to share with you this one extra special gem of an excuse I had said to me a few years ago and in all seriousness "Well you know, I would love to stop smoking cigarettes, but I meditated on this and I now know God intends for me to be a smoker". This woman felt she had come up with the ultimate validation to keep right on doing things the way she always had. I mean what an excuse! Wow!!!

THE EASIEST WAY TO LEAVE A COMFORT ZONE

This applies equally if we are afraid of going for promotion, dating, public speaking, visiting the dentist, travelling to another country, ballroom dancing, mountain climbing, spiders, reading a book, getting physically fit, having our own business, further educating ourselves, skiing, writing a CV and any of the thousand and one things which can cause us to break-out into a cold sweat at the prospect of.

Is there something you might have always wondered what it was like to do yet your self-imposed comfort zone limitations seemingly rendered this impossible?

If you live with a phobia think about when you first really experienced it, where in your personal history did you become aware of this reaction? What age were you?

If you have a fear of spiders, as a small child did you witness someone else reacting in fear at the sight of a spider?

Same with a fear of flying, perhaps you once saw photos in a newspaper or saw an incident on television what featured a plane crash? Maybe you even overheard a conversation or documentary questioning the safety of flying.

Since quite early childhood I once possessed an irrational terror of large ships. Even seeing one in a movie or documentary was enough to trigger sheer panic within me. Eventually, as an adult I decided it was time to do some tracing back through my own timeline to find the cause. After recalling when I first felt this way about ships, I realised this all originated from a children's picture book I had glanced through in year one of school (when five years old!) about Titanic and other shipwrecks. These images became lodged in my subconscious and 'protected' me from ever going near a ship, so I didn't end up sharing the same fate as those people I saw in the child's picture book. Crazy as this all sounds, for sure my story does mirror those of many who go through life fearing certain experiences or even objects, with no real knowledge of why this might genuinely be.

Finally, about twenty years ago I chose to undertake a daytrip on the very source of my fear. A large passenger ferry on a day trip to visit France; in quite rough seas as it turned out to be on the day – only to leave myself with no alternative but to have to repeat the same journey in reverse (in even rougher seas!) coming back home later that day in the evening. This experience sure cured me of that one once and for all!

And you can do the same with anything in your own life to mentally tick off another supposedly impossible task completed…

The most effective way to leave any comfort zone is to walk right ahead towards whatever is limiting you. Confront that inner demon. Tweak it on the nose a bit. Face your fear head on; and actually go ahead and do it!

I promise you the feeling is incomparable, the boost to self-esteem and confidence is worth all the temporary pain and angst. Better still you have permanently removed another barrier from your life.

To change life for the better, quite literally all that is needed is a shift in awareness of what can really be brilliantly possible and then consciously choose to go out there to make that possibility your reality.

This simple shift in belief about what is possible becomes empowering and transformational. Overcoming comfort zones places your own future directly into your own hands; any changes you choose are measured and intentionally carried through by YOU!

DO SOMETHING DIFFERENT EACH DAY

Routine is a killer to ambition. Repeating the same pattern day in day out puts us into a passive mindset of limitation. Doing something different each day usefully places us into the empowered mindset of accepting our life can also be different.

Doing something different can seem trivial, and yet pay incalculable dividends in terms of our adaptability to new situations.

Something different can be as small as:

- Driving past the usual slot here we always park our car, to go and park someplace else on the car park.
- Taking an even slightly different route on the same journey we habitually do every weekday.
- If we always head left out of the door from our place of work to go buy a bagel for lunch, turning right to sample something we have not had before.
- If we constantly wear black, putting on a red top today.
- Reading a book or doing crosswords rather watching television for one evening.
- Going to the opera mid-week or indeed any of the millions of other minor variations within our daily routine which lead us into experiencing new unchartered waters.

Getting into the habit of doing something different each day usefully also makes dealing with any unexpected stressful situations palpably easier.

Committing to even one change in daily routine ensures our subconscious becomes used to variety, then as we gradually leave behind any limiting discomfort zones, positive change happily becomes our expectation from life.

REFINING LIFE EVERY DAY

Constantly push back boundaries of what we are capable of. Improving ourselves each day in however small a way, refining how we function within our living and working environment is a magnificent way to live. These tiny adjustments every day are outstandingly self-motivating and will send your self-esteem skyrocketing once the results begin to show for you.

As one who has spent years daily looking at how I might do things better, I can tell you not only does this add to our success mindset, but it also always ensures we constantly feel inspired to achieve more.

Even if you ever feel anxious about something you are contemplating doing for the first time, go ahead anyway and jump right in, then learn as you go. None of us are born experts, this comes through experience!

Doesn't matter what and however trivial or random it might seem, every single time a small but well-entrenched discomfort zone is overcome, it further validates the fact those bigger ones can surely also be taken-on and left in the past...right where they belong.

A significant part of living life as it is meant to be is a willingness to push on regardless of any fears which well-up inside us, inner conversations of doubt trying to persuade us to make another poor excuse to stay-put. Rather than being a spectator, becoming an active participator in life. Confronting the mirages of imagined limitations; the compelling sense of inner satisfaction is incomparable. And go through the process once, next time around it is going to be easier. Start small and break down that first comfort trap, then move right on to another.

The only way we can grow is to feel that fear and take control of feeling the overwhelming sense of wishing to be someplace else. And then do ourselves the greatest service possible by going right ahead with whatever has always freaked us out to finally do it!

What Did You Say?

The results we achieve long-term depends a lot on the quality of the questions we ask ourselves when events do not go quite according to plan or when presented with challenges in life. Our goals need to stretch us to ask more of ourselves or else we stay-put exactly where we are.

If our inner questions are along the lines of "Why do these things always happen to me?" or "Can I really be bothered with all this exercising stuff?" and "I feel like having a lazy day today, how about I get up at noon?" do you imagine we here are placing ourselves in a resourceful mindset?

If we genuinely want to transform our lives, we had better start asking ourselves way more empowering questions. "What can I learn from this situation?" or "What can I do differently to achieve my fitness goals?" and "I will do whatever I need to make my health and happiness goals happen for me, however long it takes!"

WE ARE IN CONTROL OF OUR EXPECTATIONS FROM OTHERS

Bill Bolton's reputation had preceded him. Coming across his company through the wholesale business I ran for over a decade, in the trade Bill had unfortunately attracted the generally accepted reputation for being grumpy, cantankerous and abrasive in his way of dealing not only with customers but even his own staff!

I knew Bill and I might enjoy a mutually beneficial business relationship. Having talked to him on the phone, I also sensed perhaps Bill chose to be so un-user friendly as a kind of armour, a defence mechanism against the world.

Making an appointment to visit his premises, I decided as I parked my car, I would treat Bill like he was the most friendly and pleasant man I had ever been fortunate enough to meet. For the next hour I reacted like I hadn't noticed his scowl or sour demeanour. I smiled and behaved like Bill brightened my day purely for being in his company. Eventually he simply had to start reacting himself more in harmony with the open friendly way he found himself subjected to. To the utter shock of his staff Bill even laughed at a joke he made about himself!

I bought a few items from him, securing a good discount without needing to haggle. Over the next few years I would visit his warehouse once a month. Bill made a point of dealing with me personally and I believe we did become as close to friends as I think he found it possible to allow himself to be. He would drop me an email if he thought he found an item that would be in my area of interest.

My expectation did indeed bring us mutual success. Rather than believing his reputation, instead I chose to treat Bill as someone I was delighted to meet; and I think to his initial surprise, he found himself reacting in kind to me.

LIVES WE DESERVE

The guy wins big on the lottery and a few years down the line he is right back to square one, having quite effectively managed to squander and lose all of his new-found wealth. This windfall found him completely unprepared inside, lacking internal references for a success orientated mindset, and he could never feel comfortable living within the reality of being a financially rich person. His mindset being still fixed firmly exactly where it existed prior to this newfound fortune. His internal programming inevitably led him straight back into his comfort zone.

Let me share a quick story, you will understand why in a moment...

We had a family cat as I was growing-up, Fluffy she was called (because she really was very Fluffy!) When not much more than a year old she hurt a front paw and for a few days limped. There she sat holding her painful paw off the ground. I cannot begin to describe how cute she looked with one paw raised like that and such a sad look on her face. Oh, and did she ever get sympathy – treats and cuddles came her way all day long. Fluffy thankfully recovered from her poorly paw within a week or so. However, for the rest of her happy eighteen years, whenever she wanted a little extra attention or a treat, she would raise one paw off the ground and look sad. And what's more it worked every single time. Clever kitty!

Yet not too clever a mindset for us to adopt if we would prefer a life of health and happiness.

Sadly illness does also become the comfort zone of some unfortunate people. Perhaps they subconsciously enjoyed all of the extra attention coming their way when they were once unwell. We are what we focus on...we get the life we ask for every time.

How many times have you come across someone who, when we politely asking how they are, then proceed to solemnly tell you every single detail of every single ailment they are convinced they are burdened with?

Focussing on any possible avenue to wellbeing ensured my own recovery from a rather inconvenient health issue a few years back. I constantly pushed back the boundaries on what I could achieve by adopting different mindsets and refining my diet. In fact I remain convinced this personally challenging event only happened so I could learn from it to help others!

Only You Can Decide...

Neuroscience confirms we are products of the thoughts we have.

Our predominant thoughts permeate through every cell of our brain and body creating the person we are and the way we experience life. What we intensely focus on with passion creates powerful energy and scientists can physically measure this energy transmitted by our brains.

There exists a myriad of visual and aural displacements. Many people do choose to prioritise time spent in these trivial displacements rather than authentically living. Each of these displacements ultimately drags us further away from fulfilling our potential; reaching our goals.

Any time we spend locked-into one or more of these displacements results in us passively falling into inaction. And we stop all the good stuff we would love to welcome into our lives from ever manifesting for us, all because our attention is too busy elsewhere on trivia!

There are six major displacements. There are countless other minor ones, but for our purposes we will focus on the six major ones that impact so dramatically upon so many lives!

Yet there is a flip side here, we always have the choice to gain knowledge rather than lock-into displacements. We have easy access to knowledge or a displacement anytime we choose. All the time we spend absorbed in any one of these displacements ensures we opt to be passive passengers through life rather than being the captain of our own destiny...

DISPLACEMENT NUMBER ONE - READING CHOICES

The guy wakes up and before he even gets properly out there into his day he eats his breakfast while working his way through his choice of daily newspaper (or news vlog) reading all about who is killing who, which z-list celebrities have fallen from grace this week and how we are collectively heading straight into another global recession. Our guy then walks out of his front door with all this stuff running through his head. Not exactly the personally empowered way to begin his day...

What we choose to read powerfully shapes the way we perceive the world. Whichever form our reading literature takes will add to our expectations from life and influence our thinking.

Children act out the characters from their books or comics, adults are the same. As a youth, my reading choices were spy novels. Which of course influenced my thoughts and behaviour at the time – if I saw a man wearing a tuxedo, he was quite obviously a spy with a hundred concealed gadgets about his person. If someone had a generic 'Eastern European' accent they were clearly intent upon nefarious schemes ensuring global domination. Ironically I eventually fell in love with Mimi as my life partner, an Eastern European woman (although happily she seems content with her life as an English teacher, rather than attempting to become dictator of the world!).

Reading personally inspiring literature daily helps keep us on-track to our goals.

For over thirty years I have put aside some time for reading every day. If serious about personal and spiritual growth I am convinced this is essential. Even looking at my bookshelves and personal library of all the books I have already absorbed inspires me, happy all this knowledge is within me to call upon whenever required.

Our personal library is one of the greatest assets we can possess, more valuable to our future than the smartest smartphone.

Reading not only adds to the breadth of our knowledge, more crucially reading books we find personally inspirational, listening to audios or watching vids/vlogs on a day-to-day basis helps keep our actions centred upon our own self-set goals. Consciously keeping us aware of just how important all this stuff is to us.

It is all too easy to become distracted and for the mundane to take centre stage once more in our lives; studying by reading or listening to audios each day is the perfect anchor to constantly re-adjust our radar and keep our inner mojo working.

I am not going to recommend specific authors to inspire you. I believe we all need to follow our own intuition when choosing those books which are going to inspire to us. Personally I find books, vids or audios by Michael Bernard Beckwith and Jim Rohn are timeless; you need to find your own equally inspiring mentors to read. There are many more thousands of choices of self-realisation, wellbeing, and autobiographical inspirational books out there. Check them out at libraries or in bookstores and you will immediately know which ones speak to you.

DISPLACEMENT NUMBER TWO – TELEVISION AND FILMS

What we view on television is not called a programme for nothing. Everything we watch is passively programming us with usually fictional dialogue and images created by other people we do not personally know. By the way, rather alarmingly our brain does not necessarily register this experience as fictional and treats the input essentially the same as any real-life experiences!

The programmes we watch, the characters we habitually welcome into our life via television become our crowd. Just like in our real life, those main people we hang-out with we either come up or down to the same level as. Rule of thumb here is would we personally wish be friends with those characters we welcome directly into our heads via television or engage in living exactly their kind of life? No? Then quickly choose to tune into another channel or turn it off.

> Just 4 hours spent each day watching television over
>
> ONE week = **28 hours**
>
> So 28 hours every week over ONE whole month of watching
>
> television = **5 whole days**
>
> Then 5 whole days a month watching television across
>
> ONE entire year = **2 months' worth of lost days**

Imagine how amazing it would be if you were offered gratis a whole sixty extra days this year? How much further forward towards fulfilling your own dreams would you be right now if gifted those whole two free extra months to pursue your goals?

DISPLACEMENT NUMBER THREE – THE INTERNET

The internet obviously has the potential to be wonderfully informative and enlightening. There are some amazing people out there the internet affords us often direct contact with. My own personal network around the world includes incredible pioneering individuals, fellow free-thinkers one and all. Through communicating globally we ensure we are all collectively raising public awareness of the same principles. Those very same codes which have proved their effectiveness through the validation of amazing results time and time again, right down through the centuries. I am one voice; thankfully there are many more and personally I feel constantly grateful for the platform afforded by the internet, which has allowed me and my message to become globally known.

At the other end of the scale, however, a well-known car magazine recently conducted their own independent survey of the videos posted online showing any budding amateur mechanic viewers how to fix the braking system of a popular make of car. They were horrified to discover nearly 50% of the videos were either incomplete or erroneous in some way and around 10% of the advice offered, if followed, would prove to be lethal! As they commented in their editorial "Anyone with a camera can post their vid offering words of wisdom about fixing brakes, without any bona fide experience or mechanical knowledge and there is not a thing anyone can do about it". Imagine the consequences should similar health advice be followed...

Practically anyone may post anything to the internet. Right now I could start posting videos offering my totally uninformed opinions on thermo-dynamics or perhaps even more catastrophic for my viewers, run a blog giving out fashion advice!

All too often, many of us tend to unconditionally believe what we see or read on the internet, trusting that what we are reading or watching must be established fact beyond ever questioning its validity or the motivation existing behind the message.

Whilst there are some amazing websites and vlogs out there, informing and entertaining; there are also some ludicrously ignorant and seriously ill-informed people posting stuff online. Then there are those who find it amusing to intentionally misinform viewers or possess a nefarious desire to mass manipulate their followers. Well publicised court cases recently confirmed how frighteningly easy it turned out to be for these individuals to unfortunately make others take actions way outside of their own best interests.

Vloggers are fertile hunting ground for companies wanting some useful product placement, especially if the vlogger they target has enough followers. If our favourite vlogger talks up a make-up line, fashion brand, car, vacation destination, computer game, food/drink or indeed more or less any other consumer item, chances are they will be getting paid fees in exchange for the exposure. Successful vloggers do reach many millions of followers every time they post a vid, what a responsibility! Let's hope they don't have any hidden agendas as they are so well respected by our youth for their opinions...

DISPLACEMENT NUMBER FOUR – MUSIC CHOICES

Music creates feelings and feelings create our reality. The energy music gives off directly affects the cells of our body and minds. This one has been scientifically proven beyond any doubt. Famous experiments conclusively showing how various genres of music directly affects the wellbeing of plants and water molecules in a positive or negative way. Imagine how music choices will also be affecting the more sophisticated form of life known as you?

Many of us download our music directly into our heads through noise-cancelling headphones. If your pleasure involves listening to music which actually has pretty poor or unevolved messages in the lyrics, sorry to have to be the one to inform you that you are dramatically self-limiting your potential by directly programming your subconscious with trash!

I am not suggesting you need to now go and delete or sell your entire catalogue of music if you are into thrash-metal, emo bands or whatever; but you will definitely be doing yourself a great favour if you buy-out of listening to it all for at least a week and then see if you feel any different.

Inspirational contemporary music or from the amazing back-catalogue of classical composers, created with metaphysical awareness, motivates us rather than keeping us down. As with books, I am avoiding suggesting specific musical choices here, we need to trust our intuition and anyway we all have our own preferences for genres of music. And furthermore, I am convinced we really always truthfully know what is best for ourselves, even if sometimes we tend to ignore our gut instinct. I ignored mine for years with my own choice of music...

I would drive along in my car singing away to certain long-term favourite bands and what's more I already knew how self-limiting some of their lyrics were! Eventually, through the course of writing this book, I finally went through my entire music collection in a far more discerning way, discarding all of the negative stuff I did not want to programme my subconscious mind with. I had been aware of the power of music to influence our mindsets for well over three decades; walking our talk takes as long as it takes!

DISPLACEMENT NUMBER FIVE - GAMING

Computer games, such as those with brightly coloured quickly moving images designed to keep us playing on, are also stopping us from doing things to positively take charge of our life. You know the score, we are talking here about the ones widely marketed via television and pop-ups or sidebar adverts on websites, enticing us all to join in the fun to carry right on addictively playing to reach infinitely ever higher levels.

A few years ago a friend asked me to child-mind her seven-year-old boy for an hour, as she had some errands to run in the city and they would be easier to accomplish if temporarily child free. Sitting with this boy I asked him what he wanted to do and he told me he was unhappy he did not have his mum's laptop because what he really wanted to do was play his favourite computer game. I suggested instead we build something with the well-known brand of various coloured plastic interlocking bricks and begrudgingly he agreed.

Getting out the bricks to make a start, throughout our construction he constantly mimicked the noises of his favourite computer game. And I mean remarkably realistic imitations of people being shot, explosions and from time to time he would proclaim himself dead. Attempting to engage him in normal conversation was a challenge as he replied in video game speak and wanted me to join in with his acting out role-playing the different characters from his favourite game. I sensed he must have wondered which planet I had beamed-in from when it became clear to him I had no idea what he was talking about. That was one exceptionally long hour as I waited for his mum to return. And it did disturb me more than a little the level at which he partly existed all the time within this well-known game.

When I have been to parent's evenings for my stepdaughter, often the subject of computer games does come up. She shows little interest in them. Her teachers have said year after year, as she progresses through school, without exception they can always tell the children in class who spend a lot of time playing computer games, in terms of their attention span, their communication skills and the level to which they are able to interactively participate with their peers in class.

DISPLACEMENT NUMBER SIX - SMARTPHONES

Imagine creating this device which could pacify massive swathes of the population, those who live in most technologically developed countries.

These people would voluntarily spend most of their time investing their main attention on this device to the detriment of observing the reality of genuine life going on around them. Regardless of this being direct interaction with fellow humans, changes in their rights as citizens, enjoying nature, life going on in the city or indeed that truck heading right for them as they blithely stand right there in middle of the street absorbed in their screen.

Better still, how about we get the user's fingerprints/ scans of their faces/eyes as part of the process and gather all of their personal details - like who they communicate with and every email they send; who they bank with and how they spend their money down to the last penny or cent; where they are geographically located to within a metre at any given time, their interests and social media posts; if they are away on vacation and where they went; where they work or not; who they hang-out with and where they hang-out with them; what they had for lunch or even what time they usually go to bed and who with; then is all starts again when they get up the following day to eat breakfast!

And how about as part of this process we make this device so addictive to the users they consider it essential to their very survival, a vital part of their identity and day to day functioning. Their life!

Even better still, let's make the users pay out their own pockets for the privilege of being indoctrinated. Talk about a masterplan!

You really couldn't make it up...

At my talks and workshops I can virtually guarantee at some point, as I actively encourage audience interaction and a two-way dialogue, someone is going to bring up the subject of smartphones. This discussion will generally proceed along the lines of many audience members denouncing smartphones as being intrusive, time stealing and over-priced, some even going so far as to confirm they feel these devices control lives. You get the picture; the majority of those who contribute to these group discussions will have an inherent distaste for this piece of technology.

After we have talked for a little while, I ask my audience to raise their hands if they have a smartphone upon their person.

You guessed, almost 100% of audience members will put their hand up!

Then usually follows laughter. Naturally, I ask why. Their answers reveal they fear that if they don't use their smartphone they will be missing out on what their friends are up to and consider themselves to be out of the loop.

I personally don't own a smartphone. I haven't used one for over ten years now. I do possess a phone; it has just got a seriously low technological IQ. I can make or receive calls, which is about all I require it to do.

I usually bring out my own phone to show everyone at these seminars, when this inevitable subject rears its head, and there is collective amazement that a writer, broadcaster and public speaker can function with such a dim-light of a phone here in the 21st century.

I am happy to share a collective laugh at the expense of my little phone, yet I also hope it might open a few eyes. I show options, it's for others to decide what truly matters to them.

There are clinics existing in most developed countries to treat teenager's and even younger, for their addiction to smartphones. Ongoing studies by universities across the world are universally confirming that using a smartphone directly affects the user's brain.

Think about your still-developing child's brain, is even the slightest possibility of a potential harmful side-effects from long-term smartphone exposure worth the risk?

It is clearly sensible and logical for minors when out and about to be able to keep in contact with their parents and vice versa, to also communicate with their peers. How about restricting the use of smartphones to those under sixteen years old? Those younger than sixteen can still have phones capable of making calls and sending texts, but with safely mega-low electro-magnetic emissions and no direct access to surf the internet.

When we are a teenager or even in our twenties living on our phone may well seem like a perfectly legitimate use of our time…how about in our forties or fifties?

Will we be happy at fifty years old to look back and reflect upon the lost years we spent absorbed in our phones rather than building an amazing life to enjoy when we are that much further down our timeline?

I am not suggesting for one moment it is too late at fifty or even later to turn our life around. Many wonderful examples confirm that we can build an exciting new future at any point in our lives. Only would it not have been rather cooler to have already given ourselves a brilliant head start by climbing on to our personal ladder of success three decades earlier to now be reaping the rewards?

A PERSONAL EMPOWERMENT EXPERIMENT

It is all down to what we want from life. That word choice again.

The more we do anything the more engrained it becomes within our neural pathways. Yet even with the most powerfully habitual of our actions, if we stop doing them for even a short period of time, the neural pathway becomes less predominant and predeterminate to our actions.

If we replace any self-displacements with something more constructive, the chances of falling back into these old patterns of behaviour are dramatically reduced.

If you know for sure you personally buy into any of those six major self-defeating displacements, I ask you to allow yourself to indulge in a little experiment...I would like you to spend three whole days without buying into your personal choice of distraction/s. Go completely cold turkey.

"Excuse me?!"

"You're asking me to do what here?!!!"

I hear what you are saying and feel your shock. Please stay with me here, you have practically nothing to lose and might well gain something life transforming. All I ask for is only those three days commitment to this experiment out of your hopefully long life, so why not just give this one a go?

You can always go back to how you did things before once these three days are up, now a little better informed about yourself. And self-learning is never wasted.

- If you take hours devouring every word of your daily newspaper or news vlog, avoid doing this during these three days.
- Leave the TV turned off if that is your thing.
- Check emails then avoid surfing the internet if you usually spend practically every waking hour engaged on it.
- If your pleasure involves listening to music which has negative messages in the lyrics (and don't pretend you don't know exactly the type I am talking about here!) buy-out of listening during your experiment.

- Play no computer games if they usually take your attention.
- And finally use your phone only for essential communication if it is usually your life.

To make any changes stick we crucially need to replace our old paradigm with a massively more engaging new one that we can enjoy living.

DAY ONE - Okay, here we go! This first day is going to feel extremely unsettling and disturbing as you take on a radically different daily routine. Keep yourself busy doing something else, can be anything at all which distracts you from your usual distraction! Clean out a closet, have a walk, take a pen and paper to sketch something, write a poem, talk with family or friends, visit someplace you haven't been before; anything at all to occupy yourself with a positive action so you feel you are gaining from the experience.

DAY TWO - Hang on in there. This second day will probably see you constantly craving the missing element from your life. As with yesterday, be sure to keep yourself occupied and stick with the experiment anyway, after all only one more day to go...

DAY THREE - Life feels different. You held in there for two days already, how about taking a look around at what you might do long-term that you do not normally have the time for? What action can you take right now to commence making a few more long-term positive changes in your life? If you have not yet got a library of motivating books or audios, check out to see what is available. If your goals require new qualifications or skill sets have a look at what college courses exist locally or online and visit or email them to make a firm commitment. Connect to some interesting local contacts or even learn to meditate.

AKA Mistakes

All our decisions produce outcomes. These outcomes either move us forward immediately if the result is exactly as anticipated or when they do not exactly play-out as we desired, instead they help us move forward a little later. Either way we win!

Mistakes are valuable signposts, feedback from any choices we make which do not immediately produce our desired result. Rather usefully showing us the correct direction to go instead. Every mistake we make is eliminating another possible pitfall to increase our chances of reaching our goals.

Wear a mistake on our sleeves and we are judging ourselves. Limiting ourselves. Playing the negative feeling into our future, and why would we ever want such thoughts leading to nought? Got to move on, let them go and chose to appreciate the wisdoms gained. Be grateful because here is now another priceless way to avoid making similar errors in the future.

We need to develop the habit of owning our mistakes, valuing this unique opportunity for feedback. By owning them, their power to limit us in any way is gone forever.

Knowing exactly how NOT to do something is often the greatest gifts of feedback we can get, teaching us far more about the path to our goals than all the success stories in the world could ever do. We certainly all need to value them, avoid negatively dwelling on them and be grateful for the naked truths they illuminate for us!

THOUGHTS LEADING TO NOUGHT

We all encounter those temporary moments in life where we feel a little sorry for ourselves or ponder why the world is apparently not seemingly quite so fair. There are some things that come along in life we do struggle to see the upside from.

Many years ago I labelled these moments Thoughts Leading To Nought (aka stinkin' thinkin' as they have been poetically labelled by some of my fellow coaches).

Feeling this way from time to time is part and parcel of our existence as humans. We all experience them, and rather usefully we can practically choose to transform away from this frankly rather unhelpful mindset, by moving on to something more constructive.

We should never pretend we aren't having Thoughts Leading To Nought; which obviously feel extremely valid at the time. They are also usually there to show us some hitherto unknown truths about our mindset or possible better choices we could make for ourselves.

Attempting to block out our Thoughts Leading To Nought with positive affirmations, without examining exactly why we feel this way, will only ensure the next time a similar event or trigger occurs we are going to feel exactly the same way again only this time more intensely. We need to analyse why we are feeling these emotions before we may move on.

Accept that currently you do feel a little sorry for yourself and that is okay. Own the feeling. So now, what can you do about it?

Take two pieces of A4 sized paper; lay them next to one another on a table or another flat surface. On the left-hand piece of paper write down to reveal what specifically about the situation makes you feel the way you do? Perhaps the failure of well-laid plans or disappointment with yourself over the way you handled a situation. Continue until you have written down everything which makes you feel the way you do and struggle to move on.

On the right-hand piece of paper write down if there is anything at all you can learn about yourself from the fact you feel this bad? Is there something in your lifestyle or decision making sitting uncomfortably with you?

If this is the case, underneath write down step by step ways you can transform the feelings by making new choices as soon as possible. You now possess that most motivating of gifts to yourself, a set of goals!

When you are done, and you will know when you are, dispose of the first piece of paper.

Keep the other one with your new goals. Then take some immediate action to make new plans or opt for different lifestyle choices. Sometimes these transformations can be instant, other times they take a while to fully realise and show up in life, however, simply the fact you are actually taking action will stop Thoughts Leading To Nought right there in their tracks.

OR IS IT SIMPLER THAN THAT?

Or is just one of those bleurgh days we all experience occasionally? Those days when we feel overwhelmed and wonder why life cannot be a little bit simpler?

We need to accept this is how we feel, it is for sure only temporary, and everything is really okay long-term.

Re-focussing our energy is simply a matter of recalling a recent happy event we enjoyed and taking a few moments out remembering to feel a little gratitude for all the good experiences we have in life.

And smile! Create some serotonin! Stand up tall and look up!!!

Next time you are experiencing Thoughts Leading To Nought, don't beat yourself up over them or feel disappointed with yourself. Accept this is happening and choose to own the moment.

Is there something vital to learn from the experience or is it simply just one of 'those' days? Either way all is okay because occasional Thoughts Leading To Nought are ultimately only part and parcel of having a human experience on this planet.

Dedication To Meditation

I would like to share with you my personal method of meditating because I feel what I have developed can benefit you as well. My method evolved over thirty years and continues to bring new enlightenments, providing new forms of understanding along the way. All of those I have taught this method have been able to meditate practically straight away and adapt what they learned to suit their own needs.

In meditation there is no right or wrong, it is the level of understanding and personal experience or insight that ultimately matters the most. In explaining my own methodology I am merely showing a possible path. There are many other paths. If my method doesn't speak to you I strongly recommend exploring further until you find one that fits you perfectly.

If meditation happened to be taught in our schools there would be an upcoming generation of young people able to solve all of the global issues we currently face, together with automatically already possessing an empathy and compassion for their fellow humans.

When I first consciously set out on my spiritual journey of growth in the late 1980's I read hundreds of books, travelled to sacred sites and treated the whole experience as something purely intellectual to be studied and memorized. I could quote those books word for word!

Experience has taught me that the road to evolvement is experiential, requiring dedication and commitment. Sacrifices will have to be made. Yet like in all good things in life, those sacrifices are often willingly made in order for the greater understanding that ultimately results as the end manifestation.

An example would be in terms of a lot of popular culture; by this I mean most television programmes and a fair proportion of commercial radio-friendly music which jars quite significantly with my desire to reach the highest level of well-being and be the best version of myself possible. We will go further into this in the next chapter as explore ways in which the power of our words transforms how we experience life.

Negativity of others no longer affects me in the way it once did. Other than to feel a deep sense of compassion and through experience I am at able to see where their behaviour and reactions likely originated from.

How did I reach this state of compassionate, love and active detachment? Through meditation, the absolute peace of mind and inner serenity that most of us who choose to meditate feel.

THE JOURNEY INSIDE AND OUTSIDE

I would like you to meet yourself! If you have never meditated before I can tell you that this is quite an eye-opening experience.

In actuality this is a something of an understatement; it is not only eye-opening, but can be positively astounding!

If we wish to grow to any significant degree, we are logically going to have to know and understand ourselves as completely as possible. If we are sincere in our desire to heal past events, moving forward in love and freedom, what is required is a fast-track method of reaching deep our subconscious mind or inner self.

It goes without saying you are going to need to find somewhere quiet, a place that there is no chance you are likely to be disturbed. Later, as you will no doubt discover, it is possible to meditate pretty much anywhere (Trains are a favourite place of mine, the rhythm and movement of the train is a wonderful assistance for deeply relaxing) for now though finding a quiet location is essential.

You may well have seen in films or on the internet the classic meditation position - sitting on a cushion, comfortably cross-legged and with the back straight. If crossing your legs feels uncomfortable, sit in an upright chair instead and have your back straight.

Breathe steadily. In and out. Becoming aware of only your own breathing.

As you relax and feel the tension leaving your body. You are going on a journey. An inward journey to the very centre of the you of you.

Picture in your mind an elevator door. This is your own magical travel capsule. Now see the door opening and you are stepping inside. The door closes behind you. You feel very safe cocooned in your magical elevator.

You look at the numbers illuminated above the door and see that you are currently at level 0. The lift starts to move slowly upwards and you see 1 appear, then 2 as you continue up.

Becoming more relaxed with every number that passes.

With each number as you ascend you are getting closer to the real you of you. 3...4...5.

Now leaving the everyday world far behind as you continue through 6 and 7. Higher and higher past 8 and 9.

Finally level 10 is reached.

Slowly the door slides open and you venture out of your internal elevator. Time has no meaning. You are right in the heart of your subconscious. Moving with caution, start to float around and explore.

What can you sense? What can you feel? And see?

At first this is the oddest experience. Stay calm and take your time to absorb the sensations. All of your own experiences and knowledge are right here...to attempt to access all of it in one go would be unrealistic.

Simply float along and passively observe this first time.

When you feel that your journey is done for this meditation, make your way back to your internal elevator. It is right there waiting for you, as it always has been and always shall be.

The door opens and you step back inside. The number above the door is still there at level 10.

Watch the numbers as the elevator slowly automatically falls, right through back to level 0 once again, our normal waking state. The door opens. You can now open your eyes.

Congratulations you have finally met yourself!

I do know how you are feeling and it can be pretty, shall we say, mind expanding. Take a little time to allow the experience to sink in fully and then, when you feel ready, take the inward journey again. This time you feel more prepared for what to expect and can explore further. In fact, as you become more adept you can even choose to seek out certain parts of your subconscious to explore and visit...

MAKING THIS A USEFUL EXERCISE

Please be aware we all have the absolute ability to edit our subconscious. That is to jettison any of our unwanted garbage that has accumulated there. Anything that might be limiting or stopping us from getting where we wish to be is there to be exposed, ready to be cleansed.

Personally, I find the easiest way to do this is to image anything I wish to reject as a dark cloud and see it being placed neatly into an airlock I have imaged right there in my own subconscious. Now the door of the airlock is closing and the negativity is trapped right in there. There is a large red button positioned next to the airlock door and when I press it the outside door opens and then the negative thought or aspect I wished to cleanse passes out into space to be cast onto the purifying solar winds, never to return. It is done.

Meditation acts not only on the rogue thought or feeling, it also actually affects our cell memory of the event as well!

Now we know how to travel within, how do we travel outwards from into different levels of knowing and existence?

This is called journeying and as the song says...The only way out is in!

I teach guided meditation ,and in essence this is about deciding before starting out on our inner journey, what it is we wish to experience or where we wish to travel. Once the decision is made, keep the suggestion in your mind as you travel in your magical elevator and once you reach the centre of your being...push outwards.

Use your own subconscious mind as the starting point and springboard to explore outside of yourself. It is safe to do this. If at any point you feel uncomfortable or like you wish to return, all you have to do is think the thought and there you will be right back in your subconscious before your internal elevator door.

I am often asked what is possible by practising meditation and further via journeying during meditating. At the very least a deeper sense of self will be achieved, regular meditation has been proved to aid concentration and majorly de-stress. Possibilities within journeying are pretty much limited only by our own perception of possibility!

Another question I get asked is how real journeying experiences are. "Well that all depends!" is the slightly cryptic answer I usually give. There are some great master meditators who journey to physical locations in the World, subsequently being able to describe these places in intricate and accurate detail.

Equally so there are those who feel sure they are reaching higher levels of existence during their meditations, even sometimes interacting with otherworldly beings or angels during this experience; of course by its very nature this is impossible to prove or disprove; in my opinion this hardly makes the wisdoms and insights gained any less valid.

My advice is, if it feels right and your gut tells you so...99% of the time it is going to be right! I believe we all inherently know deep down if what we are doing or are about to do is right for us , and this applies in any sphere of life as well as meditation. Meditation teaches us more about ourselves and can definitely assist in learning to trust our own instinct and going with what feels right.

AND YET THERE IS MORE

I left the decision about if I should include or exclude this final section right up until I reached this point. Further to what we just talked about, my intuition is telling me that I do need to include it, for those who are ready now to take this step or for others to give them hope for the day when the allotted moment arrives when they can also undertake this journey.

We all have that part of us that is outside of the physical body. Some call this higher self, soul or spirit. Whatever label we care to place upon on, for ease of description and because this is how I personally perceive it, I am going to refer to this as our higher self.

It is possible to contact our own higher self through meditation.

There is a doorway, it exists for all who have the courage to seek it and this doorway is accessed through our subconscious mind. Seek it out during the deepest meditation and eventually you will find it.

Unless you are an Ascended Master living on Earth but are currently unaware of this fact, you will find the door to your higher self is closed.

May this door be opened, the gateway to our own divine essence? Yes, it may. You need to remain aware that to glimpse the divine is never to be taken lightly.

I am not going to tell you how the door looks. It shows itself differently for each individual. Seek it though and if you are ready, you will find it. And you will definitely know when you have!

Exercise extreme caution when attempting this. I have opened my own personal door more than once. I am going to leave it for you to discover for yourself what the experience feels like, other than to say it is like nothing on Earth! Cleansing and healing in a way that is indescribable in words. It needs to be experienced to fully understand.

I chose to share this with you as I honestly believe humanity is reaching a point in their evolution where all those who are ready need to know this information.

Those who are not ready? Well they will be unable to open the door, even if they do manage to find it, which is less than likely.

Paradoxically, at times the door to our higher self will be opened from the other side, without us being consciously aware of it. This is our higher self choosing to communicate. Those moments of pure inspiration we sometimes experience or those ideas that feel so completely perfect; those come from our higher self.

Cultivate the habit of making friends with your higher self and sincerely attempt to reach it through meditation, and those inspirational moments happen more often.

Enjoy meditation on whatever level feels right for you. Journeying will happen for you when you are ready and all the enlightenment you need personally to grow will manifest perfectly at the allotted moment for you.

So Many Words

Words are like the gears that put any of our emotions or feelings into action in our lives.

Others you engage in conversation hear but a small fraction of the entire catalogue of words you speak each day. You hear them all, every single word. You are the eavesdropper on all your private conversations, even those you are having with yourself!

WORDS WITHIN WORDS

This powerful truth bears repeating - whatever we focus on with great intensity, those thought patterns we give our attention to much of the time; makes us who we are. We are constantly creating or manifesting the life we live.

Yet our thoughts are only partly responsible, as I know by now you are beginning to realise. Words are the catalyst that outwardly expresses our feelings, the emotions relating to our current life situation.

WORDS CHANGE EVERYTHING

By consciously changing our choice of any self-limiting words, those we habitually use when describing our life or an emotional state, we possess a magical tool to completely transform that same life of ours instantly.

I AM = two of the most powerful words in existence, for those two words are always followed by a direct reference to how we feel - our emotional response to a situation or our actual wellbeing.

Whatever is added to those power words, I AM, unconditionally ensures directly exactly the experiences we have in life; our happiness, wellbeing, and success (or not!).

We use I AM to create our life when we say:

- *I am usually sad **or** I am typically happy.*
- *I am often ill **or** I am looking for ways to heal quickly.*
- *I am so bored **or** I am fascinated to learn.*
- *I am poor **or** I am successful.*
- *I am feeling old **or** I am as young as I feel.*
- *I am too shy to do new stuff **or** I am confident operating outside my comfort zones.*
- *I am weak **or** I am strong.*
- *I am undeserving **or** I am worthy of only good stuff happening in my life, learning opportunities teach me.*
- *I am furious **or** I am slightly irritated.*

- *I am unable to deal with all this **or** I am sure I will cope, there is always a way.*
- *I am utterly devastated **or** I am a little perturbed.*
- *I am deeply upset **or** I am a bit disgruntled.*
- *I am completely overwhelmed **or** I am making an action plan.*
- *I am totally lost **or** I am looking for another way.*
- *I am so full of problems **or** I am dealing with challenges one by one.*

So many times our words end up as disproportionately over-reactions to the events happening around us. For sure challenges come along in life, it happens, how we choose to describe those challenges goes a long way to us either feeling far worse or finding some inner strength to see the light at the end of the tunnel.

If we describe one of those challenging individuals we all encounter from time to time, as "Completely messing with my head" or "They make me feel sick!" or worse still "I feel like jumping off a bridge after I've been around him/her for any time!"; we quite efficiently ensure the situation feels many times worse for us than it need be. And why would we choose to do that? For sure though, so many of us do choose to buy into precisely that kind of reaction when encountering challenging people or situations.

Every time we make one of those big statements, although we may well sound theatrically dramatic and passionate, all we are effectively doing is adding massively more poor thinking energy into whatever the situation might be and guaranteeing we consequently feel considerably worse than we actually need to.

When we do find ourselves needing to temporarily spend some time around any of those people whose personal energy clashes with our own, why not instead describe the encounter as "Slightly challenging" or "A little bit irksome" or better still "I am easily able to deal with guys like that, my happiness is down to me!".

How about health issues? If we have a "Such a bad headache it feels like my skull is being squeezed" or "Now I have a debilitating flu to deal with" perhaps "Such terrible insomnia, I can barely keep my eyes open" does anyone seriously expect to quickly heal if this is how they describe how they feel?

On the contrary it is going to make us feel even less well and ensure that feeling lasts for as long as possible.

How about "Slight discomfort in my head" a "Bit of a cold" perhaps "I will take a quick power nap, then I am sure to feel better".

For some invaluable self-healing techniques see later chapter MINDFUL WELLBEING beginning on page 189.

This subject of words is so vitally important I have evolved our very own Freedom Thesaurus, to get us all thinking about the words we habitually use. Taking this as a starting point, do yourself the greatest service; choose a day to quickly jot down in a notebook any words or phrases you habitually use. Those words central to your typical descriptive vocabulary and which could well be limiting your potential. I did this myself many years ago and found myself shocked with how I described myself and my life! I wish you to have your own similarly eye-opening experience.

Prove this one for yourself by doing the exercise and using our Thesaurus. You have absolutely nothing to lose and stand to gain a lot in terms of the brand-new paradigm for living you will be creating.

FREEDOM THESAURUS

I'M SO DUMB/STUPID/AN IDIOT - If you are always putting yourself down you have personally also given the entire world the right to treat you badly!

Vitally important for your immediate wellbeing for you to permanently delete this habit from your vocabulary, especially as this produces such a negative effect upon your direct experience of life.

There is no dumb/stupid/idiot by the way - if you do not know something it is because you have yet to learn it. Does not make you stupid, simply gifts a learning opportunity to discover something new. Avoid at all costs labelling yourself dumb, stupid or an idiot. If you want to know about a subject go and find out more so you are informed. If it fails to interest you, then leave it alone and all is good! So what? There is no rule which says we need to know everything about everything. Expressing opinions on how dumb we are or how awful we look gives permission for everyone else to be critical of us as well!

I HAVE SO MANY PROBLEMS – Ouch! This is going to make anything we need to deal with seem big and scary. Some people seem to wear their challenges in life like some kind of badge of honour. We ask them how they are doing and they instantly come back with "Oh my, I have so many problems!" as they then proceed to list them, usually counting them off on their fingers as they talk. We all have things that come along in life we have not anticipated from time to time, it happens.

A new paradigm is needed if everything unforeseen is viewed in terms of unsurmountable problems. How about re-labelling them CHALLENGES? A challenge for sure brings out the best in us, guaranteeing we go on dealing with it right through to its satisfactory conclusion. A challenge is psychologically self-motivational, something to solve and see through.

MY LIFE IS SO BAD – Self-pity is incredibly self-limiting. Indulging in feeling sorry for ourselves is self-perpetuating, until we decide to break the pattern. Better interrupt this limiting mindset now by feeling some gratitude for all the things in life we so often take for granted. Like a roof over our heads, food to eat, friends and family, pets or any of the other thousand and one things we all tend to perhaps think of as ours by right, yet ought to feel heartfelt gratitude for.

Happiness always there in our own hands. How about smiling (serotonin, remember), looking up and proclaiming I AM FEELING GOOD (sounds a bit like the beginning of a cool song) or LIFE IS AWESOME!

ALARM CLOCK – Here is an example of how a small shift in a label made for a radical shift in my own attitude to my day. Every morning for quite a few years my clock went 'brng, brng' and I saw it as an alarm. Now, for me an alarm is something calamitous "Oh no, an alarm!" which set me leaping out of bed already alarmed and wondering what next alarming event was about to happen.

Eventually I realised this is silly and I re-labelled it my WAKE-UP CALL. It is still the clock going 'brng, brng' at that part of the day when I get up but labelling it my wake-up call rather than an alarm, well that is motivational "What can I do today?", it is inspirational, "That was my wake-up call, let's go see what I can do to change the world today!"

Just one small difference in the way we label something, and for sure significant changes in attitude and feelings do happen.

I'LL TRY - Trying implies making a half-hearted effort to do something. "I gave it a go, at least I tried".

To try can hardly be considered making one resolutely determined commitment to succeed whatever obstacles may cross our path; quite the opposite. Try as a word is ultimately really rather trying!

Some alternative words– I WILL DO, I AM COMMITTED TO DOING WHATEVER IT TAKES and I NEED TO DO IT AND I WILL.

IT'S IMPOSSIBLE - If the great thinkers of the past few centuries had subscribed to things being impossible, we would not have electricity, xylophones, digital watches, telescopes, surrealist art or any of the million and one other things we usually take for granted. To the closed minds of those times these great inventions or contributions to the arts must have been completely impossible. And yet they happened. Brunel, Mozart, Einstein, Mark Twain and Dali (and all the other geniuses) for sure must have met their fair share of dream stealers. Thankfully for the sake of everyone else they ignored them.

Anything Possible is ACHIEVABLE! If something is literally able to happen in any sense, it ceases to be impossible. It simply takes determination and maybe some lateral thinking for it to manifest. I am not going to suggest alternative words for this, only a beautifully open mind and a reminder of this quote from a famous movie actress and humanitarian, "Nothing is impossible, even the word itself contains I'm Possible!"

I SHOULD - Is showing a lack of real commitment. "I should wash those dishes" is not going to get those dishes washed. Should implies that for sure in theory we need to do something, but we are not really going to. Should is a cop-out phrase. I should go to University and get me some qualifications is making a statement about a possibility, without any kind of commitment. The absolute best alternative words rather than should are I WILL and even better I AM!

I HATE – Oh boy, this one makes me cringe inside when I hear it! I cannot help literally wincing to hear people start a statement with those words "I hate". So often made as a seriously disproportionally strong proclamation about something or even a person they dislike.

So many atrocities and gross acts against humanity in history have been done in the name of and justified by those two words "I hate". This phrase sends out an immensely powerful message into the universe about our way of judging situations and people. The hate energy for sure permeates through every cell of our brain and body as well. What we focus on, the energy we put out there into the universe attracts more of the similar energy back to us. When selecting "I hate" as a descriptive statement about anything, we are attracting many more situations or people to also hate into our lives. Would any of us consciously wish to bring more things to hate into the direct experience of our lives? I hope that you will agree with me when I say that I sure know I would not wish to attract anything to hate directly into my life and trust you feel the same!

How about NOT TO MY TASTE as a positively focussed statement? "She is not to my taste as a person" or "That food is not to my taste" etc,.

Of course, if there is someone or something causing us to genuinely feel for real such a radically strong reaction as actual hate, we need to remove them or it from our life as promptly as we possibly can!

I FEEL SO ILL - Is one sure way of ensuring that we are certainly going to feel worse and take longer to recover. Rather I ALWAYS QUICKLY HEAL!

EXPLETIVE DELETED – Swear words and cursing send forth such an ugly, jarring energy. And this comes straight back to the originator manifesting through their life experience. Have you ever met any habitual swearer who might be described as a role model for personal happiness?

Maintaining a cool detachment is occasionally tested to the absolute limit, particularly with certain kinds of people. Walking away may seem fine in theory, yet not always the way the situation plays out for real. What to do now then? Shout and swear? Lose control and rage? Looked at from the larger point of view of quantum reality and energy balancing, that person who caused such a strong reaction from us would of course have crossed our path. How else? If we are to grow as spiritual beings to live authentically, then we are sure going to be tested until we finally get the point of the lesson.

Alternatives to expletives OH BOTHER! OH MY! even CRIKEY! If nothing else adopting the habit of using any of these will for sure take the sting out most situations and more than likely make both parties laugh or at the very least smile. My personal choice "FERTLE THE FERTLE BURGER!" which is obviously a nonsense statement and means nothing, but allows me to express frustration in a way which makes others laugh.

I DON'T WANT - Followed by a statement of intent such as "...to be late" or "...to fail my interview" or "...to get greasy hair" might be anything. The point here is the sentence that starts with those three words "I don't want". If all of our attention is given over to arriving late, failing the interview or indeed greasy hair, that is the energy we are sending out into universe, and confirming it perfectly with our words. Guess what is going to happen next? We will be late for that interview and fail because we had to stop on the way at the pharmacy to pick up medicated shampoo and there was a queue!

More positive statements to make here would be "I PLAN TO LEAVE HOME EARLY THEN I AM SURE TO ARRIVE ON TIME" or "WITH ALL MY ENTHUSIASM I STAND A GREAT CHANCE OF LANDING MY NEW JOB" (assuming we do actually possess enthusiasm!) and "I AM GRATEFUL THAT MY HAIR IS IN GREAT CONDITION AND I WANT IT TO STAY THIS WAY".

I AM POOR - we may find ourselves temporarily low on funds from time to time, many of us have been there at some point and it rarely needs to last for too long.

In the mid-1990's I had all my capital invested in my new business which had yet to yield a profit. Looking in my wallet on the fourteenth of the month I saw just £10 and this was going to potentially be it until I made some more sales through the business. Thankfully I had already become used to thinking laterally, so I took myself to a table-top sale in a nearby village hall and bought a box containing some oldish looking vases with my £10. I proceeded from there directly to my local antiques emporium and promptly sold them on into the trade for £35, all within an hour. For nearly a year after I became an antiques trader. Buying from garage and jumble sales any pottery which seemed old and interesting, to then take along the same day to my now established network of antique dealers, happily able to usually treble or quadruple my money. As I learned more about what antique dealers look for, I organically became more informed in my buying, reducing errors and increasing my profit. Extremely useful and welcome extra income while I waited for my main business to grow into its full potential.

Poor is a state of mind that does not serve us in any way. If we don't want to go through life being poor, we had better quickly re-programme our mindset with more useful attitudes. There is always a way to turn-around temporary low funds through action, however leftfield that action might be. Now is the ideal time to put into practise some of the methods right here in this book to overcome any self-limiting thoughts and utilize your unique talents.

Avoid at any cost labelling yourself as poor! Jettison that poor mindset forever…rather more useful is I LIVE A RICH LIFESTYLE and ensure that it is, which frequently has so truly very little to do with hard cash and is way more about attitude.

IT'S NOT MY FAULT! – Making excuses for personally failing in tasks or blaming others rather than taking personal responsibility for our actions will inevitably bring along continually similar situations until we change that mindset to leave the negativity of passing-the-buck behind and be free. Lesson learned.

If we failed in that exam, then we did not study hard enough. If we got overlooked for the promotion at work we did not seem like we were ready or passionate enough for it. If we did not get that hot date with the woman/man we were attracted to, our approach was wrong or maybe they just do not fancy us, in which case it's time to move on. I ACCEPT RESPONSIBILITY FOR MY OWN ACTIONS.

I'M ALWAYS UNLUCKY - Works as a disastrous self-fulfilling prophecy. Russell is a friend who is to all intents and purposes the luckiest man ever born. He not only won on the national lottery big time, but he also then went and did it all again within a year! Every time Russell puts a coin into a slot machine, he seems to win something. He is also able to eat like he has hollow legs and never puts on a gram in weight. He constantly tells people he is lucky with money and can eat whatever he wants, never having to worry about getting fat. Russell is a fantastic example of energy in action. Russell is completely sincere when he makes those statements, in absolute belief he creates his own reality. Naturally, his focused energy and words give him precisely what he believes is true. Russell habitually says I AM ALWAYS LUCKY, and this mindset plays forward into his life.

I AM BORED – Then quite frankly now is the perfect time to engage with something to improve your life every single day!

Bored + lazy = disempowered living. Buy-into I LOVE IMPROVING MY LIFE!

PUTTING OTHERS DOWN - If we cannot think of a nice think to say then say nothing, as the old saying goes. Putting others down always says far more about us than the victim of our words. Would we really wish to be known as insecure and cynical? That is how those who put others down come across, every single time. And untrustworthy as well! Would we impart anything of importance to someone who gossips or says negative things to us about mutual friends?

RETHINKING OUR WORDS THAT ARE HEARD

We are able to consistently find opportunities to refine our habitually used vocabulary. Here we are presented with such a fundamental method that anyone one of us can employ to immediately improve our quality of life in ever such a simple way.

155

AFFIRMATIONS

Meditation helps here. When I started with affirmations a few decades ago I found the best time to say them was directly after my meditation. I would have a few postcards with my chosen affirmations written down on them placed by the side of me, when I finished my meditation, I would be in the correct mindset to contemplate saying some affirmations.

If you find, for the moment at least, you cannot get into the right mindset for affirmations (and they need to be completely relaxed and never from desperation) best avoid using them. You really will not be doing yourself any favours and on the contrary, they can be more limiting to yourself, rather than achieving anything worthwhile.

Mindset and feeling are all that really matters to unlock the way to attract anything positive for ourselves and the words we then choose to use that reinforce that feeling. Followed by directly getting involved in the nuts and bolts of making the process real, when the time becomes obvious for taking some action.

If you are going to use affirmations, you vitally need to feel the emotions first. Before a word comes of your mouth begin to build up the feelings inside of you. Build it up and build it up and build it up. This REALLY matters to me! I need this in my life, this reality in my life!!!

And only then say the affirmation...whilst still being prepared to take the necessary action that is our part of the deal!

You do not need to chant it three thousand times. Once a day is plenty with all this powerful emotion, the feeling behind those words of yours!

As I have already written more extensively about this in my book Staying Positive Regardless I am not going to suggest specific affirmations here or exact words or phrases, because I trust you will know what is relevant in your life and what will work best for you.

So far we have dealt with ways to live more in harmony with ourselves. How about experiencing amazing health as well?

A Long And Healthy Life

Our human body is the only physical means we have at our disposal to enjoy this amazing bluey green planet of ours!

It makes perfect sense then the fewer stresses we put on our physical body and digestive system by choosing carefully what is taken into it, the easier time it is going to have.

Personally I have found during the course of the last three decades plus of studying how my own body reacts to what I choose to nourish it with, it functions better by giving it mostly unprocessed food. The more natural my chosen food stuff is, the smaller the list of ingredients on any kind of label gracing the packaging, the healthier and happier my body is.

Eating food free from artificial colours/sugars, flavour enhancers, e-numbers and artificial preservatives means our delicately balanced digestive system is going to have an easier time coping with it.

So many of us tend to eat as regular as clockwork and this can leave us feeling either hungry, in those times when we are burning those extra calories or else overfull, because we ate when the clock told us it was time for lunch, even if we didn't actually feel like it right now.

Develop the habit of eating when hungry, rather than when the clock insists it is our mealtime. This is listening to the needs of our body and places far less stress on our digestive system.

Grazing throughout the day; eating a little often, gives our digestion an easier time by never stressing it. Further on this subject, overburdening our body and this applies even with the healthiest food or drink if we overeat, is putting unnecessary strain on our finely tuned digestive system.

ANOTHER CHOICE

As someone who then lived the urban life, the invitation to spend a few days staying right in the heart of the country on the poultry farm owned by my extended family was an opportunity I readily jumped at.

We seldom realise beforehand those pivotal moments which happen in life, this was to be just such an experience.

Arriving late at night, the following morning I got the guided tour of the farm, consisting of shed after giant shed of caged battery-hens. Entering the first shed to witness first-hand the stark reality of the confined life of these hens left me shocked and horrified. Over the next couple of days of my vacation I occasionally ventured solo to peer into the sheds, observing more closely, but only from the safety of the doorway. If you have never seen such a place, let me tell you the stench and sound is overwhelming, that combined with the sight of tens of thousands of tightly caged birds ensured I left after a few days, to return to my life resolutely vegetarian and seeking to know more.

A vegetarian diet uses about 25% of the land required to feed a meat eater annually. For a vegan it is only 20%. Of two identical areas of land, one purely for rearing cows and the other given over to vegan food, the vegan plot will feed up to five times as many people. This crop will also require a minute percentage of water needed by the cattle, and of course, none of the methane our bovine friends produce (adding to greenhouse gasses) will be produced by that field of wheat!

Vast areas of land, including the rainforest have been or are being cleared to rear livestock for consumption. Over half of the grain produced in the world is used to feed livestock; of which but a small proportion (some estimate as low as just 10%) could instead be used to feed all of us across the world.

Having become established as a vegetarian, I later graduated to vegan and am currently macrobiotic vegan, through listening to my intuition during a recent journey to self-healing.

I attribute much of my ongoing wellbeing to also becoming entirely free of sugar or artificial sugars in my diet; more of which shortly.

I drink plenty of water (but not too much) and get plenty of exercise. If I cannot get out and take a walk (my favourite form of exercise) I ensure to make the effort to have a 15-20-minute aerobic work-out with weights at home each day. A few years ago, I decided it would be a good idea to take myself off to my chosen healthcare provider and get a full physical. As a validation to myself I am doing things right. Imagine my delight when she told me I have the physiology and level of fitness of a healthy twenty-five-year-old (I am not twenty-five).

BROWN RICE

This does have a bit of an image problem here in the West, I get that. Brown rice has become a little synonymous with VW campervans, the tie-dyed hippie movement and free love. I love hippies by the way; I have been labelled The Hippie Holistic Coach by the press on more than one occasion due to my uncompromisingly approach to wellbeing and more than likely, my bohemian appearance.

The simple truth is pure brown rice benefits one and all. In the Far East brown rice is an essential part of the diet. This ancient grain is one of the purest foods we can eat. Naturally high in fibre, brown rice still contains all those essential vitamins and minerals which get removed when it is processed to make white rice.

I recommend this staple of the macrobiotic diet, regardless of your own dietary lifestyle. Brown rice added into weekly meal plans, ensures you are taking into your body one of the most natural foods on the planet.

Eating not only brown rice, but other natural grains such as whole-wheat, rye and barley and avoiding refined white flour or synthetically processed foodstuff, ensures we fuel our bodies in the purest way. Combined with fresh vegetables, beans and pulses we eat as holistically as possible.

VITAMINS

We have easy access to just about every and any type of possible vitamin, mineral or supplement conceived of or imagined. All we need to do is hit any high street or go online. Yet how many of these vits do we genuinely need to be taking and how many are simply passing through our bodies serving little useful purpose or even physically harming us?

During the last thirty years or so I confess, as a health aware vegan, I must have sampled at one time or another pretty much every of the myriads of different vitamin and mineral concoctions available; the promised goal being to replace the essential elements vegans apparently miss out on through avoiding meat, dairy and fish.

The message here is vits are easily obtainable and we are all free to self-diagnose. If you do genuinely feel you could use some extra vitamins over and above your usual diet, take the time to go and get checked by your chosen healthcare provider. That way you are sure to be supplementing with vits or minerals you genuinely need short term. Then take the care to look at what could be added into your diet for the long-term fix.

If you are veggie or vegan, it is practically mandatory to have your B vits checked periodically as a matter of course and for peace of mind. A nicely balanced diet might well render further supplementation obsolete.

The other point we need to bear in mind is our needs are more than likely going to be entirely different during the summer months as opposed to winter, if your instinct is you would benefit from supplementation, a visit to your choice of healthcare provider allows you to know for sure. Facts when it comes to our wellbeing are always preferable to guesswork!

SUGARS

And so finally we arrive at the subject of sugar, the avoidance of which in any form has become one of my own personal passions!

I need to qualify before we start this section, I am not a nutritionist, and whilst we all need to develop the habit of listening to the needs of our own bodies, nevertheless before contemplating any extreme dietary changes it is wise to firstly consult your chosen healthcare provider.

And now back to sugar...

Too many refined, artificial or even natural sugars which are added into thousands of the things we eat is asking a lot from our bodies to be able to absorb these alien substances which have only really become such a high percentage content of our diets in the last fifty or sixty years.

There's an excellently researched book called Sugar Blues by William Dufty; although written back in the 1970's, its continued relevance today cannot be understated. If serious about wellbeing I do recommend you read this or a similar book.

Sugar causes highs and lows in our moods. And yet so many of us are unaware of just how many refined sugars we are taking into our bodies every single day. Sugar is added to practically every single processed food. Even if you think you might well be enjoying a low-sugar diet, check out all those ingredients and you will find virtually everything does indeed contain sugar or artificial sugar concealed under one name or another.

COMMONLY USED NAMES FOR SUGARS AND SUGAR ALTERNATIVES – Aspartame, Syrup, Fructose, Saccharin, Sucralose, Sorbitol, Glycerol, Dextrose, Concentrated Fruit Juice, Galactose, Corn Syrup, Ethyl Maltol, Glucose Syrup, Maltodextrin and Barley Malt; there are literally hundreds of chemical and e-numbers manufacturers of foodstuff and cosmetics use in place of simply stating sugar on their list of ingredients.

Sugar gives us that familiar high. It contains absolutely no nutritional value whatsoever, but it certainly does give us a high. That energy rush, unfortunately shortly afterwards comes the crash. Then we feel lacking in energy. Yet not only does sugar affect us physically, it directly influences our moods.

Wendy felt incredibly down and lacking in motivation a lot of the time. Digging down into her life revealed nothing of any real consequence which might be causing her to feel this way. She had no health issues or stresses beyond what most of us experience. I followed my intuition to suggest to Wendy she might like to adjust her diet for a minimum of two weeks by cutting out as much sugar and artificial sugar that she felt comfortably able to. She duly reported back after this fortnight she felt like her life had been transformed, experiencing a sense of being so much more in control of her emotional wellbeing and balanced in her moods.

Ponder deeply sugar, by all means research it online - but first a word of caution. Be sure to read from reputable sources, a fair percentage of the online 'research' relating to sugar has been rather sneakily funded by a certain global high-profile soft drink manufacturer. Not exactly unbiased advice! Shame they aren't as public in admitting the phosphoric acid used in their soda is made out of horse urine; still as it only makes up 10% of the content of their popular soda I guess that's all okay…

After looking into sugar and its side effects, you agree with me this is not something which ought to be part of your diet – start to gradually reduce your sugar intake. Don't go cold-turkey and cut it completely out of your diet, gently easing away from sugar will put far less stress on your body.

As part of my own healing journey a short while ago I decided overnight to abruptly adopt this no sugar and free-from artificial sugar lifestyle. Convinced as I personally was, through paying attention to clues from my body, sugar had contributed greatly to the health issues I found myself dealing with. This left me with no choice; I had to go cold-turkey. Having experienced that particular rollercoaster I can share with you gradually reducing our sugar intake is for sure the gentler way of doing things!

If you too go sugar free, you are going to soon feel the difference in your life. There will be a period of withdrawal, stay with it anyway and persist until your body is cleared of all those processed sugars.

I wake in the morning energized and have the most amazingly balanced moods/emotions I have experienced at any time in my life.

ORGANIC

There is organic food and then there is ethically produced organic food.

Some of the animal waste based organic fertilizers, such as chicken pellet manure commercially used by growers and directly available to us via garden stores, has been produced as a by-product of factory farming in one form or another. This might be okay for many people; however, with the broader picture of ethics taken into consideration, feeding our plants with the by-product of a brutally efficient system of farming can hardly help us to grow happy botanical specimens.

The same applies with pesticides. Rather than drenching our food in chemicals like most commercial growers do, there are more natural ways of doing things. Permaculture is an example, the planting of sympathetic plants to protect one another from likely pests. Using essential oils such as citronella as a repellent to avoid crops being eaten by insects or lavender to discourage weeds are becoming more widespread. There is a wealth of reliable information on the internet from organizations such as The Soil Association and a version of the Organic Consumers Network exists in one form or another in most countries.

If you are buying most of your foodstuffs in from grocery stores, a little personal investigation into where their products come from and how they are grown can pay dividends. Alternatively, growing your own fruit and vegetables puts you in control of what products go onto them and happily there is a wealth of ethical organic options out there, either for fertilizing or pest control.

Caution Poisonous!

As we have already established, us humans are creatures of habit. And unless we get some kind of clarion wake up call, the chances are whatever neural pathways we have taken years to establish will continue to run the same programmes and patterns throughout our lives.

Many people do indeed spend small fortunes to self-inflict poisons upon their bodies in the full knowledge of the potential negative side effects of their lifestyle choice.

The only reason any of us continue with an action which is clearly against our self-interest is because we have not yet given ourselves a sufficiently good enough reason to not do!

Please understand I am not judging anyone's actions. I am a passionate advocate of our right to complete freedom of choice, obviously as long our actions harm no others. And yet paradoxically some of the lifestyle choices we make for ourselves do indeed unintentionally have an all too real and sometimes devastating effect on those who love and care about us.

I feel particularly motivated to encourage any of you who do buy-into one or more of the following health-defeating lifestyle choices to look within yourself for your personal **Good Enough Reason** to change. Get your inner health mojo working in your own behalf in your own life; you can thank me later!

Every one of us already knows about all the self-inflicted poisons we are soon to be talking about. My wish is that we all now collectively achieve a different level of personal understanding through talking candidly about them.

I need to add ,if you are addicted to any of these self-inflicted poisons be sure to take the advice of your chosen healthcare provider before making any changes; there is so much support and help available, take it all if you feel that you need it!

During each section I will detail one or two of my own personal **Good Enough Reasons** and suggest some emotional levers you can also use to bring a new paradigm to transform an old habit.

SMOKING

I am a bit of a non-smoker; well okay I never felt inclined to try it. As I mentioned, I am passionate about the freedom to make our decisions, mine has been to avoid tobacco. I personally always disliked the aroma of smoking, which was been enough to put me off ever wanting to become a smoker. Throughout my childhood I could not eat if someone nearby smoked, and to be candid I still feel the same way today!

It has been known for certainly all of my lifetime that smoking is hardly beneficial to health in any way. On the contrary it creates as a by-product its own range of serious health problems and issues with the ingested carcinogens. I believe we are all responsible for our own actions, and in these times in which we live, everyone is fully aware of the health risks involved in choosing to smoke. The packaging on tobacco carries brutally graphic illustrations of the damage we will inflict upon our bodies when smoking, but this alone is not enough to persuade the passionate smoker to quit.

We all need Good Enough Reasons to change a habitual behaviour. If you are doing everything else right and still smoking, you already know you are making your body work so much harder to clear the associated toxins.

Cigarettes also contain sugar, this surprises many people, they indeed have remarkably high sugar content, up to 20%. Clearly health hazards need to be considered relating to a high sugar intake as well!

My mother had not smoked for well over two decades, but unfortunately as a previously heavy smoker the damage was already done. She died five years ago due to (amongst a few minor secondary issues) complications from her years of smoking; even though she had not touched a cigarette for so long. I can confirm for you, having been alongside her all the way, death from smoking is agonisingly slow and excruciatingly painful.

At an event I met a woman in her early twenties who during her lifetime had witnessed her great grandmother, great grandfather, grandmother, and tragically both of her parents all die due to smoking related cancers and bizarrely she also smoked! Clearly, she had yet to encounter her personal Good Enough Reason to make a new paradigm. No matter how much logic and common sense says otherwise or the emotional pain we experience; we are quite able to turn a blind eye to changing habitual behaviours so deeply embedded within our neural pathways.

The most effective way to transform any poor habit is to link pain or self-ridicule to it.

Take some photos of yourself smoking; really study these photos to see how incongruous with living a long and healthy life this action is.

In most first world countries, being a smoker in winter means standing outside in all weathers any time you feel the need to indulge. Take photos of this; standing outside shivering in minus temperatures or attempting to shelter from the gale force winds and icy rain, while you enjoy your smoke. See for yourself how switched on and intelligent you look...

Volunteer at your local hospice, freely giving of your time to help others, whilst also witnessing first-hand the far from beautiful final period of life endured by those with cancer caused by smoking. Find your own Good Enough Reason to quit.

We will go more into how crucial it is to replace any poor life-choices with something more pleasurable at the end of the chapter...in the meantime, let's talk...

ALCOHOL

Often considered fine in moderation, some health experts even going so far as to suggest that a glass of excellent quality organic red wine or beer is health beneficial. A good rule of thumb is if we avoid overburdening our body with anything that requires a recovery time from eating or drinking we are on the right track.

During my brief encounter with the biggest publishing company in town during my first job, I met two engagingly witty salesmen, Tim and Larry. They were both kind to my sixteen-year-old self and spending some time laughing with them certainly brightened the few dull weeks I spent at that company. After I left, we still crossed paths occasionally, but sadly not for too long. Tim and Larry were both functioning alcoholics; they had seemed old to me when I was sixteen, but in reality were only in their mid-forties when liver disease claimed both of them within a few months of one another. Consequently, since then my personal association with alcohol etched into my belief system, is the premature ending of life. My Good Enough Reason is an over-riding emotion relating to alcohol that it robs us of authentically living life to the full, as epitomized in the case of my two late friends whose intellect had burned so brightly.

The guy finally gets his long sought-after promotion at work or is about to get married the next day. Cue taking on-board industrial quantities of alcohol to celebrate the occasion. This one has mystified me for years; surely some awesome news worth celebrating is a time to savour? Rather than making it into an occasion we will more than likely not actually remember or perhaps would even prefer to forget!

To change any habit we need to transform the emotional way we view it, how it makes us feel. Having photos of ourselves to reflect upon are wonderfully eye-opening!

As I suggested with smoking, if you habitually over-indulge in alcohol be sure to take plenty of selfies during the process of becoming inebriated. The following day take a good long look to study just how you looked and behaved during the previous evening.

Better still take photos of how awesome you looked waking first thing in the morning after that heavy night before! When you are on your way for another night-out keep one particularly stinking photo of what alcohol does to you as the home-screen on your phone as a poignant reminder to yourself.

We only need to check-out any news blog or newspaper to read of the latest family to have been devastated by alcohol, through a drunk-driver or someone passing away far before their time (as with my two friends) due to liver damage.

If you drink every day it is worth considering that you could well have an issue with alcohol. To confirm this go for three days without touching an alcoholic drink. If this is a struggle or turns out to be impossible, seek out what support or help is available locally.

JUNK FOOD

This is not called junk for nothing! An occasional junky indulgence our bodies just about cope with. Living off the stuff constantly is inevitably self-damaging. Deep fried food is universally recognised by nutritional experts as increasing the likelihood of heart disease, high cholesterol and diabetes. Moderation or avoidance all together must be the sensible option for any of us interested in a long and healthy life.

Food products are generally advertised in terms of the lifestyle eating them will offer. Not much attention on the product, it is far more about the cool happy people in the adverts who are having a wonderful life and all because they eat the advertised food or soft drink.

I met Shane after he had already suffered a serious heart attack, he was burdened with diabetes and grossly overweight. His career as an airline I pilot far behind him through his physical health issues, nevertheless Shane still found it challenging to eat healthily, claiming junky food gave him pleasure. Frankly seeing where his eating habits had taken him it was more challenging for his family and friends to understand exactly what pleasure he derived...we all have a choice.

Junk food is packed full of flavour enhancers such as MSG, e-numbers, sugar in its myriad of forms, and artificial colours to make it look more attractive. Is it any wonder wholefoods and more natural dietary options can seem a little bland comparatively? We need to reset our taste buds. If we do this after a short while purer eating will begin to taste delicious.

As a teenager I indulged in junky delights. I can confirm that gradually transforming the way we eat does indeed also change the way we taste food in a positive sense. I guess you have to give this a go to experience it.

My Good Enough Reason came through the irrefutable visual evidence of how my energy levels increased, and the way my skin and hair looked after cutting out poor quality foodstuff sand switching over to a more natural way of eating.

In youth our bodies recover from over-indulgence in poor foodstuffs quickly, although the results are generally still there in dermatological evidence or cholesterol levels.

It bears remembering that according to Zen every front will have a back, therefore if we spend our youth eating and drinking junk, somewhere further down our timeline payback day will arrive. This could manifest as later in life being faced with serious health issues we now need to deal with, those which might have been easily avoided with different lifestyle choices earlier.

If you know your diet consists of a greater proportion of highly processed or junk food, why not take yourself off to your chosen healthcare provider for a full physical examination? Ask them to not only test for the usual stuff such as cholesterol, body mass index and vit levels; also find out the condition and real-time age of your skin through dermatological profiling and your level of physical fitness.

RECREATIONAL DRUGS

Offer an artificial form of escapism. Regular users of recreational drugs claim their habit does no harm. Medical statistics would say otherwise. Long-term use of recreational drugs can affect us through psychological issues such as creating paranoia, difficulty in concentrating and if over-used death!

There is a tradition within artistic and creative endeavours for some to use so called soft drugs as a means to access ways of expanding their consciousness (as shamans traditionally also do to enter other realms). Yet how real are the results of all this artificially induced music or art? The guy who cannot get artistically inspired without smoking drugs must not be naturally a creative type of person...meditation equally also allows us to expand our conscious awareness...

Far too many amazing singers and actors have been lost to drugs. All the commercial success they attained and adulation of the public failed to fulfil their emotional needs and they chose to ease their pain through drugs.

If you have children and want to raise awareness in them about the reality of drugs, get them involved in donating food or clothing to a drug rehab centre. Make it your family centred project, then all of you visit the rehab centre to personally give them your donation, allow your children to see first-hand the stark reality of drug use.

If you are a creative person who extensively uses drugs as a part of your artistic process I am going to get a bit in your face to call you out, and challenge you right now to see what you produce without any artificial high. You might well surprise yourself...

CAFFEINE

Coffee gives us an energy rush, increases our heartbeat and too much caffeine causes stomach upsets. In my corporate days I would regularly drink over twenty cups of coffee a day! Not surprisingly I suffered from insomnia and irritability daily. A routine blood-test showed up practically caffeine running through my veins, definitely my overdue wake-up call and Good Enough Reason to adopt an instant new paradigm!

Too much caffeine risks many more possible side-effects than we can cover, you know the ones we are talking about –kidney issues, high blood pressure; and painful withdrawal symptoms such as cluster headaches.

I recently enjoyed a detailed conversation with a brain surgeon who stated neither he nor any of his colleagues drink coffee or caffeine rich drinks. Enough validation for any of us against caffeine I would say...

YOU DESERVE TO FEEL AWESOME!

Feeling personally motivated is essential to make any kind of change in life. We need to link pain or better still self-ridicule related to continuing with our existing paradigm. I cannot tell you exactly what's going to push your buttons; you are going to have to work that one out for yourself...

What we can all do though, when deeply desiring to transform away from indulging in any type of action we unconditionally know makes no sense at all (such as intentionally self-poisoning) is to firstly get our inner health mojo working for us.

And secondly replace the negative action with something awesome we would love to do instead.

This feel-good action can be anything that feels amazing to you; walking within nature, making love, getting a pet, spending quality time with family, studying something new, taking up woodwork, origami, writing poetry, volunteering of our time, going to the gym, swimming, travel, cooking deliciously healthy meals, running or meditating.

When we actually improve our quality of life by taking on something new we love to do as part of the process of discarding an old paradigm, we gift ourselves the best possible opportunity for our desired changes to stick.

An Exercise In Wellness

As our body matures it is usual for it to start losing muscle mass, to be replaced with fat or muscle wastage, resulting in less physical strength and suppleness.

It does not have to be this way, not at all.

The only reason for this loss of muscle mass is due to a lack of aerobic and anaerobic exercise - our brain then receives the message that we are not using muscles in the way we once did and concludes we must no longer require them. Kick-starting the transformational changes in our bodies commonly recognised to be signs of old age.

Yet there are many examples of lean and mean octogenarians who are still superbly fit and leading the kind of active lives that would put many of their grandchildren to shame.

What is the difference here, what can possibly be their miraculous secret?

In virtually all these cases those individuals have always led active lives and saw no reason to slow down or stop doing what they have always done simply because another birthday passed on by. As a result of this, they have kept a good high percentage of their muscle mass throughout their life.

GETTING OUT WHAT WE PUT IN

Exercising is crucially important for maintaining a healthy body and strengthening our immune system's ability to fend off disease and decay. Investing in ourselves, eating healthily and partaking of regular exercise, is going to be more than worth the effort later down our timeline when we can still run up the stairs and experience life to the full.

I spent my time in gyms back in the day and for sure they are an excellent starting place when venturing into getting fit for perhaps the first time in years. Any good gym will have qualified instructors to advise you on taking those first steps. It is vital to start gently at first. If you realistically know you are extremely unfit, it is certainly prudent to consult a health professional before beginning to make any changes.

Regular gentle exercise is always preferable to doing nothing at all, and you can always increase the length and intensity of your work-out once you start to gain enough fitness to safely feel more able.

Small steps towards our goals are preferable to none every single time!

NEVER NEED TO DIET

It seems every week a new miracle diet hits the headlines, with the usual promise of quick weight-loss by buying-into their incredible new eating regime.

Give or take a kilo, I have weighed the same for the past three decades. This is not because I might not be inclined to put weight on; it is all down to firstly eating holistically with an eye to my long-term wellbeing. And secondly, also making sure my lifestyle includes plenty of aerobic exercise for fitness and some anaerobic exercise for muscle mass.

Rather than buying into yo-yo dieting, completely tailored lifestyles for holistic wellbeing gives us the best chance possible of maintaining our perfect weight long-term.

We are what we focus our attention upon, what we think about and say makes our reality. If we are spending every day desperately obsessing on the need to lose weight and frequently glancing in the mirror underlines this, for sure we need to quickly adjust our mindset to experience the difference this makes. If all we constantly think about is losing weight, we will constantly have weight to lose – adopting a new mindset will prove significantly more effective and work more permanently than any diet. We need to re-apply all our attention on building our lifestyle around actively becoming our vision of how we see our ideal physical self.

We empower ourselves by opting to turbo-charge our weight loss goals with the right mindset; and consequently designing a tailored lifestyle to bring ourselves to where we desire to be physically, this is the only skill-set needed to achieve genuine permanent weight loss.

This is so easy as well!

Quite simply cut out of your new lifestyle anything at all incongruous with how your vision of the way your ideal self looks. Choosing to focus all your attention on things such as tastily fantastically healthy food/drink and taking regular exercise. Find an exercise you buy-into and really enjoy, this can be anything from dancing, yoga, swimming, martial arts, running, zumba, hill trekking or taking part in a sport, something you look forward to doing and can easily be integrated into your weekly routine.

Make this choice right now and you bring this vision of your ideal physical self that much closer into genuinely being your long-term reality. Quite rapidly you will see the results manifesting for you, ensuring your lasting motivation to carry right on all the way through to finally living the life you deserve and feeling good about your mirror image...

OUR NATURE TO BE FOUND IN NATURE

Nature is good for the soul. Our ancestors lived a life far closer to nature. They were aware of the passing seasons and how to read coming weather changes.

Is it any wonder given our usual fast-forward lifestyle so many in the 21st century have lost an inherent spirituality?

I am not necessarily talking about organised religion here. I mean more looking within ourselves and thinking about who we fundamentally are; our interconnection to the infinite. Why we are here on this planet in this moment...

We deserve to engage with life to the full and enjoy every single day, whatever twists and turns it might take, remaining true to our own ethics and moral code.

Enjoying some fun, this might well cost absolutely nothing in hard cash, but is nevertheless priceless. Now that is really living!

- Think of walking in a forest during a fresh shower of rain, those heady scents combined with the sound of birdsong high above in the trees.
- Sitting by a seashore as roaring waves crash in onto the beach or perhaps soothingly lap gently onto the shoreline.
- The beauty of taking in the awe-inspiring wonder of a meadow resplendent with a kaleidoscope of wildflowers.
- The drama of a wild thunderstorm.
- Looking up at the eagle majestically soaring against a stunning sunset.
- To be out on a cold crisp winters evening, the sky purest black and a million stars twinkling like diamonds.
- Or a scorching hot summer's day, feeling the sun warming upon our backs and experiencing true contentment.

This is real life.

This is directly appreciating freely given beauty, the beauty of nature, of our own natures; and it is all waiting right there as it has always been. Waiting for you and me to feel it through all our senses, with every breath down through every atom of our very being!

So, what would you rather enjoy?

Any one of those amazing natural experiences or spending more time on your phone?

Why not go and take a walk instead?

Living 24/7 in completely artificial environments stifles creativity and deadens our intuition. Creating an uninspired zombie-like worker-drone level of existence.

If you are one of those people who doesn't usually have the time for nature or perhaps even finds the prospect of exploring wilderness areas scary, how about you take only half an hour a couple of times a week to visit your local public park?

Simply sit and observe. Leave aside the headphones and no cheating yourself out of the experience by talking or texting on your phone!

Look at the trees, the grass and then listen. Hear birdsong? Do the trees make a noise? Rustling poplars or creaking old oaks. Breathe in the scents. Soak up the sights, sounds and smells, feel on every level what it is like to be there.

Like we cannot step into the same water of a river twice, every time we visit nature it will be different.

Slowly, but surely, your awareness of nature will grow more acute through these visits to the park. Eventually even venturing a little further outside the town or city, to explore untamed nature. Then again, perhaps you are already very connected to nature and cannot relate in any way to this section so far, living as you do in the country or on the edge of an area of wilderness.

Oh, you can help so many people!

Invite your town or city family and friends to come over to stay with you as if possible. Show them your reality. Take them outside and allow them to learn to appreciate the joy of nature through your eyes. Be their guide and show them how beautiful nature is in all her manifestations.

Exercise in nature is my first choice every time. Walking, running or tai chi within a natural setting is far from taking exercise – it is wonderfully inspirational. Most of my game-changing ideas popped into my head way out in the wilderness or in the middle of a deserted ancient Neolithic site. Rarely do I feel connected to nature enough to feel inspired in the middle of a busy city...

As I lead a fairly public life, my way of finding some battery re-charging time is taking myself off for an all-day solo coastal walk or deep down into the forest. This is especially effective in the heart of winter when the harsh weather discourages many others from venturing outside. It is for sure a challenge in this era in which we live to find ourselves some true seclusion. I have to say though, a gale force wind and driving rain usually means I am going to enjoy having the beach pretty much to myself and with the magical bonus of making me feel wonderfully alive, leaving me with a heart full of gratitude for nature in all her extremes.

Take the time to take some time out for you – there is always a way.

Mindful Wellbeing

There is an old saying - image, ordain and manifest.

In other words, think about something deeply; keep that image strongly focused there in your mind. Then say it out loud and the energy wave transmitted makes it happen for you. And it still holds 100% true.

Phil's greatest fear was losing his mind. Having witnessed his much older brother succumb to dementia, Phil dreaded the horror of his own life following the same path. Although he was perfectly fit, ate for optimum health and led an extremely active lifestyle, he nevertheless fixated upon the unlikely chance of developing a similar illness. For sure his brother had died through this illness but this hardly compelled Phil to also go ahead and experience the same fate. By fixate, I mean he read everything there is to know about the subject, often verbally expressing just how much he did not want to get the illness or lose his mental faculties.

Sure enough he did eventually find his life turned upside down. Phil did not get dementia, sadly though he did develop a benign but inoperable brain tumour. With only a few short months of life ahead of him, Phil did finally make the connection between the thoughts of fear he had vocalised for years and where he now found himself. Did Phil's thoughts attract his illness? He told me he was certainly convinced they had...

At the other end of the scale, the energy from our own thoughts can bring about little miracles.

Another guy I know also found himself diagnosed with a growth in his brain. He first noticed it the persistent headaches and soon cognitive challenges manifesting as quite noticeable short-term memory issues. Eventually taking himself off to get checked by his chosen healthcare provider revealed a colloid cyst lodged in the centre of his brain. Three separate specialists in turn had 'the conversation' with him, explaining the position of the cyst meant it would be inoperable; inevitably it would grow and eventually lead to sudden death with no warning.

Our guy quit work for a while, not to wait for his imminent demise, but rather to work on himself every single day through meditation, refining his dietary input and visioning living a future of his own choice, free from pain or limitation. It took him three years of continuously empowering mindsets as he gradually re-gained all his cognitive faculties, his once poor short-term memory now fully functioning again, the debilitating cluster headaches passed to never return. He leads a significantly fuller and richer life than ever before his diagnosis; and with a renewed passion for experiencing new things wherever and whenever possible.

ALL HEALING IS ESSENTIALLY SELF-HEALING

If we go along the conventional route to health, taking ourselves off to a GP and embracing orthodox medicine, it is still essentially our own body which is healing for itself. Prescribed drugs or medication simply will not work if we believe they are not going to be effective. Conversely there have been well documented cases of individuals making full recoveries from illnesses or injury, while having been taking nothing more than a placebo pill, their trust in its effectiveness being strong enough to bring about healing.

Our mind is immensely powerful and possesses infinite capabilities to heal our bodies...we simply need reminding how and we can grow into our full potential. In the rest of this chapter I will show you some naturally holistic techniques to deal with a few of life's little health challenges.

I do need to add a word of sensible caution before we carry on; obviously these techniques are not intended to act as a substitute for the attention of your chosen healthcare provider. If you are feeling persistently unwell do always seek professional help.

THIRTY SECOND DE-STRESS

I want to give you something which, although never intended as a long-term solution, represents an instant way of taking ourselves away from a stressful situation, calming things down to re-centre and look at whatever we need to deal with more within context.

Perhaps it is one of those days, one challenge after another presented itself and we feel like we are about to go pop!

How to do it...

- Sit still and close your eyes.

- Concentrate on the colours you can see behind your eyelids, even if this is black, no rules here. Whatever colours you see is fine.
- In your mind start to count slowly back from 30 to 0.
- 30 (pause and breathe) 29 (pause and breathe) 28 (pause and breathe) 27 and so on, until you eventually reach 0.
- When you have arrived down at 0, you can open your eyes.

Many people, from all walks of life, have found this simple little exercise incredibly useful. It is something I have been teaching for over twenty years and everybody who has adopted it into their lifestyle has found some degree of benefit from it.

The beauty is the Thirty Second Destress may be practiced almost anywhere at any time. I mean clearly when it is safe to do so – if you are driving please find somewhere safe to park-up first or if operating heavy machinery do move away before using this exercise!

On a more serious note though, do feel free to share this once you have proved to yourself that it works. The more people who know about the Thirty Second De-Stress the sooner we can collectively bring a little more peace into this World...

By taking this opportunity to go within ourselves for a few moments we psychologically disconnected from the immediate cause of the stress there before us. Like I suggested, this is never intended to be a long-term cure, what it does though is place our personal power back into our own hands, rather than feeling events are running out of control. When feeling more centred we are for sure able to deal with any possible challenges we find ourselves presented with in a level-headed way.

When teaching others, my primary aim is for my audiences or clients to be able to quickly take complete control of their own lives and destiny. What would be the point in anyone relying on someone else to solve all their issues for them whenever a challenge in life happens along? Far better we all develop the inner strength and confidence in our own ability to deal with whatever crosses our path.

INSOMNIA

Sleep is essential if we are to function to the best of our ability. Sleeping when we feel tired if at all possible. Sleep is regenerating.

When suffering from insomnia, and we have probably all been there at some point, for sure I have, can seem unending! There are some methods we can use to help us enjoy a good night's sleep.

- A crucial step is to avoid coffee or any caffeine rich drinks for at least four hours before retiring to bed. Drink something else, chamomile tea is excellent, very relaxing. Have a chamomile tea an hour or so before you are contemplating retiring for the night.
- Take a warm shower. Leave aside any invigorating shower gels, instead something more relaxing to put you in a chilled mood. A nice warm shower, with calming shower gel will place you more in the mindset for sleep.

- Essential oils can help as well. Never put them directly on your skin. Place a few drops of lavender essential oil (if you like the aroma) on a handkerchief or tissue, put this under your pillow where you are able to smell it, but it is not overpowering, helps the mind get into a more relaxed ready-for-sleep state.

- I have found one of the methods which works well for me is to hypnotise myself to sleep. Which in my case, is to start at one thousand and gradually slowly count backwards to zero in my head. I do generally find long before I have even reached back to nine hundred, I am fast asleep!

RELATIONSHIPS

If our relationship is the cause of stress, honesty with how we are feeling and frankly communicating this is so freeing. Especially if this can be discussed without resentment or hostility.

Firstly, we need to be honest with ourselves about what we truly feel. And once we have gone through the process of searching within, we can begin to share this. Let's face it, if our relationship is the cause of feeling stressed, then in all likelihood our life-partner is going through a similar reality and will likely welcome the opportunity for dialogue.

Sitting down and talking with one another is the beginning to resolution. Resentment builds up through a lack of communication and if everyone knows exactly where they are, at last some kind resolution can happen.

You now both transparently see where the relationship is going to go and how to move forward.

Keep talking to one another, even if these discussions happen over the course of several days or even weeks; seek counselling if you mutually believe it will help. Talking may potentially bring you closer, as you understand one another's needs a little better now. Then again, if you collectively reach the conclusion that the relationship is genuinely not fixable then you can both amicably let it go, allowing each other to be happy elsewhere.

HEADACHES

Wouldn't it be rather wonderful if there were a truly holistic way to self-heal a headache? Often related to stress, but not always, headaches can be one of the trickiest maladies to self-heal. After all, we need to be able to focus our attention to help ourselves and a challenging pain in our own head is clearly going to make this a particular challenge to overcome.

As one who used to find myself subject to headaches regularly and unwilling to pop a pill to ease the discomfort, I sought out a method to help myself whenever the need presented itself. One which by necessity did not require many hours of focussed concentration or meditation on my part.

Find somewhere quiet to sit, with no bright lights to distract you or electronic gadgetry in your proximity.

- Close your eyes and intensely focus your attention directly on the area of pain (don't worry, this won't be for long!).
- Strongly imagine the pain of your headache as this grey cloud floating outward from your forehead, to hover in the air a metre in front of you.
- Your headache pain, now floating in the air right there on level with your head a metre away.
- Then watch as it slowly commences moving away from you, drifting away into the distance until you can no longer see it.
- Open your eyes, if you have done this right, you will be feeling considerably more at ease now.

I need to add that this method is obviously not infallible and if you are experiencing persistent headaches, please do take yourself off to your chosen healthcare provider to get assessed.

I have to say this is one of the most popular self-healing techniques I teach, giving people their own ability to treat their headaches has proved invaluable to them.

PAIN

Dealing with pain from a physical injury; or specific pain in an isolated area of our own body, works by precisely the same methodology as the previous section on headaches.

- In the same way as with our headache, strongly tune-into the epicentre of the pain to FEEL the discomfort.
- Then image it as a grey cloud lifting away from the area of your body which the epicentre of the pain is centred, to float a metre or so in front of you...
- And as before, the grey cloud drifts away to eventually disappear.

If you have a persistent injury it may well be useful to practise a healing session per day for as long as it takes to dissipate entirely.

Like with the headache healing, here we helped ourselves by taking the element of a localized pain; and symbolizing it as a grey cloud moved it outside of our body.

HOLISTIC THERAPIES

There are a whole range of therapies which can help us relax more to deal with stress and emotional blockages.

An aromatherapy massage is wonderfully soothing. Most towns have an aromatherapy clinic, find one with the official certifications and insurance hanging on the wall and book a session. You will surely feel better for the experience, it costs extraordinarily little proportional to the relaxation achieved.

Acupuncture and acupressure work on the meridians of the body, releasing any emotional energy blockages which could be causing our physical symptoms. Deep tissue massage and reflexology are infinitely calming.

It is worth the effort for seeking out an alternative therapy which speaks to you, if sensing you could benefit from outside help. Recommendation are always the preferred way to choose a therapist or counsellor, ask friends or look online to know more about a particular therapy or practitioner.

Start From Where You Are

Whatever your starting point in life, the desire to improve your reality takes only passion, investing in some love, and some drive to make it happen. The Universe does not care if we come from a family of twelve children with parents who struggled to put food on the table or were born into the most privileged circumstances – background is unimportant when daily living goals.

Having the clearest vision of where we are going, being awake to opportunity, we ensure we are going to we arrive. Energy is energy and works in thankfully the same way for us all.

ABOUT THE JOURNEY

We need remember to remember this. Although the ultimate destination is wonderful, also taking the time to enjoy the process of living each day throughout the journey of getting there ensures we remain motivated to achieve ever more.

When you see some those long-held wellbeing and happiness goals realised, and by following the steps throughout this book you certainly stand a good chance of them finally coming into your life, other dreams organically proceed to take pride of place as future goals.

It really does never end and indeed quite right too, it truly never needs to!

And remember anything you want from life that is literally physically possible in any way at all must by its nature become achievable, now here is the true essence of The Magic of Holistic Living!

Brightest Blessings

Dean Fraser

About Dean Fraser

I began my quest to learn more about human potential well over three decades ago. Taking a year out from my corporate life, I read hundreds of books, travelled to visit ancient sacred sites and networked with fellow seekers of wisdom from around the world. I qualified in Body Language Psychology which acted as a springboard to my life's quest to help others discover the reason they incarnated on this beautiful planet of ours at this time. I never returned to the corporate world. Each year I write for thirty magazines across the world on ways of living in harmony and wellbeing with ourselves.

www.deanfrasercentral.com

Karma is Quantum Energy

Dean Fraser

Walking Our Talk Is Easy, Right?

Powerful stories to awaken your inner mojo

Dean Fraser

Printed in Great Britain
by Amazon